Laurie Blum's FREE MONEY Series

Childcare/Education

FREE MONEY FOR DAY CARE

FREE MONEY FOR PRIVATE SCHOOLS

FREE MONEY FOR FOREIGN STUDY

FREE MONEY FOR COLLEGE

Health Care

FREE MONEY FOR HEART DISEASE AND CANCER CARE

FREE MONEY FOR DISEASES OF AGING

The Arts

FREE MONEY FOR PEOPLE IN THE ARTS

Business

FREE MONEY FOR SMALL BUSINESSES & ENTREPRENEURS

HOW TO INVEST IN REAL ESTATE USING FREE MONEY

Other

FREE DOLLARS FROM THE FEDERAL GOVERNMENT

1992-1993 Forthcoming Titles

FREE MONEY FOR CHILDHOOD BEHAVIORAL AND GENETIC DISORDERS

FREE MONEY FOR INFERTILITY TREATMENTS

FREE MONEY FOR MENTAL/EMOTIONAL DISORDERS

Laurie Blum's

FREE MONEY

for Children's Medical and Dental Care

A Fireside Book
Published by Simon & Schuster
New York   London   Toronto   Sydney   Tokyo   Singapore

FIRESIDE
Simon & Schuster Building
Rockefeller Center
1230 Avenue of the Americas
New York, New York 10020

Copyright © 1992 by Laurie Blum

FIRESIDE and colophon are registered trademarks
of Simon & Schuster Inc.

Designed by Christina M. Riley
Manufactured in the United States of America

1 3 5 7 9 10 8 6 4 2

Library of Congress Cataloging-in-Publication Data
Blum, Laurie.
[Free money for children's medical and dental care]
Laurie Blum's free money for children's medical and dental care.
p. cm.
"A Fireside book."
Includes index.
1. Child health services—United States—Endowments—Directories.
2. Children—Dental care—United States.   I. Title.
RJ102.B58   1992
362.1'9892'00973—dc20   92-509
CIP
ISBN 0-671-74594-8

· · · · · · · · · · · · · · · · · · · ·

I would like to briefly but sincerely thank my
"A Team," Christina Riley, Deborah Brody,
and Fori Kay, as well as my wonderful editor
Ed Walters, and of course Alan Kellock.

Contents

· · · · · · · · · · · · · · · · · · ·

Foreword

• •

by **Richard L. Saphir, M.D.**
Clinical Professor of Pediatrics,
Mount Sinai School of Medicine

When I began a Pediatric practice in the sixties, money was plentiful, and medical and hospital costs were relatively inexpensive. People with some form of income could usually afford care for themselves and their children. As inflation and then recession came along, and medical technology went through advances and introduced consequent escalated costs, it became increasingly difficult for many families to afford medical care for their children. Major businesses that provide health insurance for their employees cut their budgets for health care, and/or provided medical insurance that would cover less and less. Children who, for some reason, were on Medicaid or Medicare, were provided for, at least to some extent, but patients with somewhat higher incomes (those who were not eligible for governmental aid) were squeezed financially. Parents of children with special needs, including a wide variety of developmental disabilities and chronic illnesses, found particular difficulty in obtaining affordable, long term care.

In this country our infant mortality rate has declined at a much slower rate as compared to other nations. It is important to note that every developed nation in the world, other than the United States and South Africa, provides health insurance for all children. 38 million Americans are without any health insurance coverage, and children represent the largest segment of the uninsured population — an estimated 12.2 million children under the age of 18. In addition to lack of insurance, many children are underinsured. Medical insurance and health insurance frequently provide only major medical and catastrophic coverage (and often with high deductibles).

What happens to the families and the children whose tremendous medical expenses exceed their insurance coverage? What happens to the families who fall outside the aid of governmental agencies for health care? Access to care for all has been a prime concern of the American Academy of Pediatrics, but we are far from producing the type of care or medical help that many families need and deserve.

Laurie Blum has succeeded in accumulating an amazing group of funding sources — to help parents pay for their children's medical and dental expenses. It is truly amazing how many sources are available for funding, sources that one would not know had they not read this book. A dividend for those of us who read this book is healthier babies, healthier children and reduced out-of-pocket costs. I offer my congratulations to Laurie Blum for accumulating this information, and for making it so readily available to all of us.

Introduction

. . . .

Health care spending is expected to rise by 11% to $817 billion in 1992. Health care spending is rising about 2.5 times faster than the GNP; one out of every seven dollars in 1992 will be spent on health care. It surprises no one that medical costs have increased — and continue to increase — not only at a rate faster than the growth of the overall economy, but higher even than the rate of inflation.

What does surprise many is the extent to which American consumers pay directly for their own and their children's medical care; total out-of-pocket costs reached $175 billion last year! American consumers pay directly for 29% of the nation's total medical costs for a number of reasons. Some 38 million people, many of whom are children, have no health insurance; one-third of all those who are uninsured in America are under the age of 18. Those families that are insured still pay a portion of routine medical expenses because of deductible and coinsurance provisions. And yet it is children, along with the elderly, who need access to regular medical care.

Free Money for Children's Medical and Dental Care directs readers to the billions of dollars available annually for both short- and long-term medical and dental care. Much of the available money is awarded without regard to the financial status of the recipient, and none of it ever needs to be paid back. The book includes information on funding available in all fifty states.

The book is divided into six chapters:

1) **"Associations: Funding and Referral Information"**
(listing child health care foundations and associations that
provide a wide range of services, including: supplying
information; sponsoring and referring patients and their
families to clinics and support groups; and providing
physician and dentist referrals, funds for research, and
patient services);

2) **"Private Foundation Funding"** (listing possible sources
for monies for direct medical expenses, such as doctor/
dentist fees, prescription costs, and hospital bills);

3) **"Corporate/Employee Grants"** (listing companies and
corporations that provide grants for the medical care of
their employees' children);

4) **"Flow-through Funding"** (providing information about
foundation monies that are given to individuals through
sponsoring nonprofit organizations);

5) **"State and Regional Government Grants"** (including
local state health care offices, as well as native health
service grants, which provide funds for American Indians
and Native Alaskans); and

6) **"Federal Grants"** (identifying agencies offering direct
funding and/or essential referral information).

Where possible, listings within each chapter are arranged
state-by-state to make this book as easy to use as possible.
Check your state's listings in all six chapters to see which
grants or corporate programs apply to you. You'll find
funding parameters and an address and phone number to
contact for further information (and application forms).

By the time this book is published, some of the information
contained here will have changed. No reference book can
be as up-to-date as the reader or the author would like.
Names, addresses, dollar amounts, telephone numbers, and
other data are always in flux; however, most of the information will not have changed.

While reviewing this data, readers are advised to remember that funding sources are not without restrictions and that researching, applying for, and receiving aid will take time, effort, diligence, and thought. You are going to have to identify the source of aid for which you qualify and determine whether or not you fulfill geographic and other requirements. You are going to have to fill out applications. You may meet with rejection and frustration somewhere along this road. The odds, however, are in your favor that you will qualify for some sort of funding assistance.

On the next pages is a concise, how-to guide to writing a grant proposal. Follow my instructions and you should be successful in obtaining some sort of assistance. Good luck.

How to apply

As indicated by the number of listings in this book, thousands of resources for health-related funding exist throughout the country from government, private foundation, and corporate sources. Applying for this aid is the challenging part; it requires diligence, thought and organization.

First is the sorting out or research/gathering phase. Look through each chapter of the book and mark each potential assistance source. Pay close attention to the listed restrictions and qualifications, eliminating from your list the resources least likely to assist you.

Then, politely contact each of your listed sources by mail or phone to verify all current information, such as address, telephone, name of the proper contact, and his/her title (in cases where the contact's name is not listed, begin your letter, "To Whom It May Concern"). At this time, you can also arrange to get a copy of the source's most current assistance guidelines, and an application form if one is required. Use this opportunity to find out about any application deadlines and to ask where you are in the funding cycle (i.e., if there is no deadline, when would be the best time to apply; also, be sure to ask when awards will be announced and funds distributed). However, do not "grill" or cross-examine the person you reach on the phone. Always be prepared to talk about why you are applying and what you are applying for — in case you ring through to the key decision maker, who decides to interview you on the spot!

Second is the application phase. Most often you will be asked to submit a formal application (rather than a proposal). Always be sure to read (and follow!) the instructions for completing the application. Usually the same material used for one application can be applied to most, if not all, of your other applications, with a little restructuring to make sure you answer each and every question as asked, appropriate to each application.

Grant applications take time (and thought) to fill out, so make sure you give yourself enough time to thoroughly complete the application before its deadline. Filling out the application can be a lengthy process, because you may be required to write one or more essays. Often, what is required is a "statement of purpose" explaining why you need the assistance for which you are applying. You may also need time to assemble required attachments, such as tax returns and other financial records. (Don't worry, in most cases, you won't be penalized for having money in the bank.) You may also be required to include personal references. Be sure to get strong references. Call all of the people you plan to list, and ask them if they feel comfortable giving you references. Remember, you have to convince the grantors to give money to you and not to someone else.

Be clear, concise and neat! You may very well prepare a top-notch application, but it won't look good if it's been prepared in a sloppy manner. Applications (and proposals) should always be typed and double-spaced. Make sure you keep a copy after you send off the original — I have learned the hard way that there is nothing worse than having the funding source be unable to find your application and your having to reconstruct it because you didn't keep a copy.

You should apply to a number of funding sources for grants and awards, as no one application is guaranteed to win an award. Although none of the sources listed in this book requires an application fee, the effort you will have to put in will probably limit you to a maximum of eight applications (if you are ambitious and want to apply to more than eight sources, go right ahead). Remember, the more sources you apply to, the greater your chances for success.

COMPONENTS OF
A SUCCESSFUL PROPOSAL

One of the largest categories of grants that are given to individuals are grants for general welfare and medical assistance, that is, "free money" for emergency or long-term personal, medical or living expenses. The various funding agencies that make these awards have happily made applying for these grants much simpler than for other categories. Most, if not all, of the foundations to which you will be applying will require the following in order to consider your request for funding:

1. A brief but concise letter outlining your child's medical problem and/or the expenses and bills you have incurred. In the final paragraph of your letter, you should specify a dollar amount that you feel confident would ease your financial burden (i.e., "I request a grant in the amount of $2,500 to help me pay the costs associated with a visiting nurse, which is not covered by my medical insurance"). Remember to look carefully at the "$ Given" information in the listing for the foundation to which you are applying; if the foundation only gives grants ranging from $5,000 to $15,000 and you need $20,000, you should request only that amount which the foundation gives.

2. A report from the doctors or hospital staff involved with the child on whose behalf the grant request is being submitted. Because of the enormous volume of mail that most foundations receive, you may want to get the medical reports directly from doctors and/or hospital personnel and submit them with your application. This way there is no chance that a foundation can delay or turn down your application on the grounds that it is incomplete.

3. A copy of your tax return. Don't panic! You will not be penalized for showing excellent earnings or for having savings. The issue is how the costs associated with the medical problems or care requirements with which you are faced alter your financial stability. However, if you are in financial need, you will certainly be given every consideration.

4. A personal interview. This may take place by phone or in person. Stay calm. Foundations are run by people committed to their mission of helping those in need or in trouble. Simply state the facts of your case and all will go well.

Remember, your application should be clear and concise. Your letter should not exceed two pages. Be sure to include any attachments the foundation might require, such as medical reports and tax returns. Follow my instructions and you should qualify for some sort of "free money."

Associations:
Funding and
Referral Information

This chapter is an invaluable resource guide for the patient and his/her family. It contains listings of foundations/associations that address the needs of individuals with specific diseases. Among the many services they provide, these organizations publish information about the disease, sponsor and refer patients and their families to support groups, give physician referrals, and award funds for research as well as for patient services. Though not all of the foundations/associations offer monies to be paid directly to patients, I felt it was imperative that I include this information in this book. Having experienced catastrophic illness firsthand, I know all too well the comfort and support that a professional association offers the patient and his/her family, who are frightened and overwhelmed.

The chapter is divided into six major categories: Associations, Wish Fulfillment Organizations, Special Health Care Facilities, Support for Families Experiencing the Death of a Child, Associations and Services for Children with Disabilities, and Mental Health Associations and Services. Within these categories, sections are organized alphabetically by names of diseases or disorders. The various associations/foundations are listed alphabetically under the name of the disease or disorder they address.

Patients and their families will probably find, as I have, that the various staff members of these foundations/ associations are exceedingly helpful during difficult times. Use them and their associations to your best advantage.

ASSOCIATIONS

. . . .

ASSOCIATIONS

GENERAL HEALTH

American Academy of Pediatric Dentistry
211 East Chicago Avenue
Suite 1036
Chicago, IL 60611
(312) 337-2169

Description: Professional society of dentists promotes pediatric dentistry through practice, education, and research.
Contact: Dr. John A. Bogert, Executive Director

American Association of Public Health Dentists
10619 Jousting Lane
Richmond, VA 23235
(804) 272-8344

Description: Society of dentists, hygienists, health educators, and others actively involved in public health dentistry.
Contact: R. Gary Rozier, President

Association for the Care of Children's Health (ACCH)
7910 Woodmont Avenue
Suite 300
Bethesda, MD 20814
(301) 654-6549

Description: Provides brochures (free or for a nominal fee) focusing on the emotional needs of parents and children during a health-care experience.
Contact: Beverly H. Johnson, Executive Director

Child Life Council
7910 Woodmont Avenue
Suite 300
Bethesda, MD 20895

Description: Promotes psychological well-being and optimum development of children, adolescents, and their families in the health care setting.
Contact: Christine Brown, President

Children in Hospitals
56 Bellows Hill Road
Carlisle, MA 01741
(508) 369-4467

Description: Offers advice to parents on how to find sympathetic doctors and hospitals. Distributes list of published articles, including: We Learned Through Our Son to be Wise Medical Consumers and Parents: Consider Yourself Part of the Health Care Team.

Children's Defense Fund
122 C Street, N.W.
Suite 400
Washington, DC 20001
(202) 628-8787

Description: Publishes a book (priced at $12.95) examining the factors that affect infant health, as well as providing information about state and federal benefits programs.

• •

Federal Hill-Burton Free Care Program
(800) 638-0742 Hotline
(800) 492-0359 MD

Description: Provides free or low-cost medical care at 2600 participating facilities. Call for a free brochure describing eligibility requirements.

Health Resources and Services Administration
Office of Public Affairs
Department of Health and Human Services
5600 Fishers Lane, Rm. 1443
Rockville, MD 20857
(301) 443-2086

Description: Publishes and distributes a directory listing all Health Services Administration publications.

National Association of Community Health Centers
1330 New Hampshire Avenue, N.W., Suite 122
Washington, DC 20036
(202) 659-8008

Description: Promotes continued growth and development of community-based health care delivery programs for underserved populations; disseminates information and research data.
Contact: Thomas Van Coverden, Executive Director

National Institute of Child Health and Human Development
National Institutes of Health
Department of Health and Human Services
9000 Rockville Pike
Bethesda, MD 20892
(301) 496-5133

Description: Provides up-to-date information on such topics as developmental disabilities, birth defects, and sudden infant death syndrome.

National Institutes of Health
Consumer Information Center
Department 140X
Pueblo, CO 81009

Description: Publishes *Parent's Guide to Childhood Immunization*, a booklet explaining how vaccines protect children from eight serious diseases and identifying possible side-effects of these vaccines. Booklet also includes immunization schedules. Send $1.25 for a copy of the booklet (140X).

ASSOCIATIONS

• • • • • • • • • • • • • • • • • • • •

**National Vaccine
Information Center**
128 Branch Road
Vienna, VA 22180
(703) 938-3783

Description: Provides referrals to support services; reports adverse reactions related to vaccines.

**ODPHP National Health
Information Center**
P.O. Box 1133
Washington, DC 20013-1133
(800) 336-4797

Description: Provides callers with names and addresses of appropriate organizations; refers health-related questions directly to such organizations for answers.

Pediatric Projects, Inc.
P.O. Box 571555
Tarzana, CA 91357
(818) 705-3660

Description: Distributes medically-oriented therapeutic books and toys for children undergoing health care. Provides parents with material about helping children cope with illness, disability, medical treatment, and hospitalization.

**Sick Kids Need
Involved People**
216 Newport Drive
Severna Park, MD 21146
(301) 647-0164

Description: An association of professionals and families interested in specialized pediatric home care for technology-assisted and medically fragile children; identifies resources available to families and aids them in gaining access to those services.
Contact: Karen A. Shannon, Executive Director

AIDS

**Department of Health
and Mental Hygiene**
AIDS Hotline
101 West Read Street
Suite 825
Baltimore, MD 21201
(800) 638-6252

Description: Refers callers to testing sites and counseling services; toll-free number statewide within Maryland.

Public Health Service
AIDS Hotlines
(800) 342-AIDS

Description: 24 hours a day, 7 days a week; (800) 243-7889
Description: Voice/TDD; Monday-Friday, 10a.m.-10p.m. Eastern Standard Time; (800) 344-7432
Description: Spanish; 7 days a week, 8a.m.-2a.m. Eastern Standard Time

4

• • • • • • • • • • • • • • • • • •

Terrific Inc.
Grandma's House
1222 T Street, N.W.
Washington, DC 20009
(202) 462-8526

Description: Provides support for children with AIDS in the forms of: service, care, preventive education, and housing for children with AIDS in Washington, DC.

ALLERGIES

American Academy of Allergy and Immunology
611 East Wells Street
Milwaukee, WI 53202
(800) 822-2762

Description: Distributes free literature on allergies — including asthma, hay fever, eczema, food allergies, and hives — that can affect children's health and learning abilities. Send self-addressed, stamped envelope. The Academy also provides referrals to local allergy specialists.

American Allergy Association
P.O. Box 7273
Menlo Park, CA 94026

Description: Distributes information on food allergies, diet, environmental control, etc. Send self-addressed, stamped envelope.

Asthma and Allergy Foundation of America
1125 15th Street, N.W.
Suite 502
Washington, DC 20005
(800) 7-ASTHMA
(202) 466-7643

Description: Provides practical help nationwide, with publications (*What is Asthma? What is Allergy?*), written referrals, medical/social rehabilitation for chronic asthmatics, and outpatient allergy clinic.

National Institutes of Health
Consumer Information Center
Department 126X
Pueblo, CO 81009

Description: Distributes pamphlet, *Pollen Allergy*, which explains common pollen allergic reactions, treatments and research. Send $1.00 with specific request for the pamphlet (126X).

ASSOCIATIONS

· ·

**National Jewish Center
for Immunology and
Respiratory Medicine**
Lung Line
1400 Jackson Street
Denver, CO 80206
(800) 222-LUNG
(303) 355-LUNG within
Denver metropolitan area

Description: Uses trained nurses to answer questions about
the detection and management of such lung-related
problems as asthma, emphysema, chronic bronchitis,
tuberculosis, juvenile rheumatoid arthritis, and allergies.

ARTHRITIS

Arthritis Foundation
2307 Chapline Street
Wheeling, WV 26003
(800) 479-5044 within West
Virginia
(304) 232-5810

Description: Provides literature related to treatment and
prevention of rheumatic diseases.

**National Jewish Center for
Immunology and
Respiratory Medicine**
Lung Line
1400 Jackson Street
Denver, CO 80206
(800) 222-LUNG
(303) 355-LUNG within
Denver metropolitan area

Description: Uses trained nurses to answer questions about
the detection and management of such lung-related
problems as asthma, emphysema, chronic bronchitis,
tuberculosis, juvenile rheumatoid arthritis, and allergies.

ASTHMA

**Asthma and Allergy
Foundation of America**
1125 15th Street, N.W.
Suite 502
Washington, DC 20005
(800) 7-ASTHMA
(202) 466-7643

Description: Provides practical help nationwide, with
publications (*What is Asthma? What is Allergy?*), written
referrals, medical/social rehabilitation for chronic asthmatics,
and outpatient allergy clinic.

• • • • • • • • • • • • • • • • • • •

Mothers of Asthmatics
1075 Main Street
No. 210
Fairfax, VA 22030
(703) 385-4403

Description: Helps parents deal with the practical aspects of raising a child with asthma; offers a support system and advice on problems of asthmatic children.
Contact: Nancy Sander, President

National Jewish Center for Immunology and Respiratory Medicine
Lung Line
1400 Jackson Street
Denver, CO 80206
(800) 222-LUNG
(303) 355-LUNG within
Denver metropolitan area

Description: Uses trained nurses to answer questions about the detection and management of such lung-related problems as asthma, emphysema, chronic bronchitis, tuberculosis, juvenile rheumatoid arthritis, and allergies.

BLOOD DISEASES

Children's Blood Foundation, Inc.
424 E. 62nd Street
Room 1045
New York, NY 10021
(212) 644-5790

Description: Exists to support the Division of Pediatric Hematology Oncology at The New York Hospital-Cornell Medical Center, the premier pediatric hematology/oncology facility in the U.S. Here children receive comprehensive care for such blood diseases as hemophilia, thalassemia, leukemia, sickle cell anemia, ITP, retinoblastoma, and AIDS.

BURN INJURIES

National Burn Victim Foundation
308 Main Street
Orange, NJ 07050
(201) 731-3112

Description: An association of physicians specializing in burn treatment and others interested in burn treatment and care; provides a 24-hour emergency burn referral service and a crisis intervention team made up of professionals who provide counseling for burn victims and their families, to address psychological problems and physical handicaps remaining after treatment.
Contact: Harry J. Gaynor, President

ASSOCIATIONS

• • • • • • • • • • • • • • • • • • • •

CANCER

American Cancer Society
1599 Clifton Road, N.E.
Atlanta, GA 30329
(800) ACS-2345
(404) 320-3333

Description: Distributes free booklets and videotapes for children in treatment, and for siblings and parents of children in treatment. Titles include: *What Happened to You Happened to Me; Mister Rogers Talks about Childhood Cancer;* and *Back to School — A Handbook for the Parents of Children with Cancer.*
Contact: Local unit of the American Cancer Society; check telephone directory listings

Association for Research of Childhood Cancer
P.O. Box 251
Buffalo, NY 14225
(716) 681-4433

Description: Funds the expansion and continuation of research in pediatric cancer centers and provides seed money for pilot projects in cancer research; provides support to parents of children with cancer.
Contact: Charles Moll, Executive Officer

Cancer Information Service
National Cancer Institute
Building 31
Room 10A24
9000 Rockville Pike
Bethesda, MD 20892
(800) 4-CANCER
(800) 422-6237

Description: Hotline provides information on prevention, diagnosis, treatment, and confidential counseling services.

Candlelighters Childhood Cancer Foundation
1312 18th Street, N.W.
Suite 200
Washington, DC 20036
(800) 366-2223
(202) 659-5136

Description: Offers guidance and emotional support for families of children with cancer and identifies patient and family needs to enable medical and social systems to respond adequately; provides 24-hour crisis lines, babysitting, and transportation services; sponsors blood and wig banks, immune programs, and the establishment of Ronald McDonald residences for families of children requiring extended care away from home.
Contact: Julie Sullivan, Executive Director

• • • • • • • • • • • • • • • • • •

**Corporate Angel
Network (CAN)**
Building One
Westchester County Airport
White Plains, NY 10604
(914) 328-1313

Description: Nationwide program providing cancer patients with available seats on corporate aircraft to travel to or from recognized treatment. No cost to the patient; no financial-need criteria. Available seats cannot be guaranteed; backup reservations must be made. Request CAN transportation when a definite date for appointment or discharge has been set.
Contact: Judith Haims, Administrator

**Leukemia Society
of America**
2900 Eisenhower Avenue
Suite 419
Alexandria, VA 22314
(703) 960-1100

Description: Provides leukemia patients and families with information, phone counseling, and literature; collect calls accepted. Financial aid awarded to qualified outpatients being treated for leukemia, lymphomas, and multiple myeloma and Hodgkins disease.

Make Today Count
101 1/2 South Union Street
Alexandria, VA 22314
(703) 548-9674

Description: Brings cancer patients and their families and neighbors together to discuss openly the false implications and the realities of life-threatening diseases; stresses a positive approach to the problems of serious illness in order to lessen the emotional trauma for all concerned; helps professionals to communicate with and meet the needs of seriously ill patients.
Contact: Sandra Butler Whyte, Executive Director

**National Institutes
of Health**
Consumer Information Center
Department 523X
Pueblo, CO 81009

Description: Publishes a free pamphlet, Healthy Tanning – A Fast-Fading Myth (523X), which presents the symptoms of skin cancer and stresses the benefits of protecting the skin.

Skin Cancer Foundation
245 Fifth Avenue
Suite 2402
New York, NY 10016
(212) 725-5176

Description: Publishes and distributes literature, posters and charts on the prevention of skin cancer. Makes available the latest information on sunscreen products that prevent skin cancer.

ASSOCIATIONS

. . . .

DIABETES

American Diabetes Association
505 8th Avenue
New York, NY 10018
(212) 947-9707

Description: Provides educational material on early detection and management to the public, as well as to diabetics.

Diabetes Research Institute Foundation
8600 N.W. 53rd Terrace
Suite 202
Miami, FL 33166
(800) 321-3437
(305) 477-3437

Description: Provides specialized patient care and comprehensive educational programs for health professionals, patients and families. Recognized worldwide for excellence in clinical research; working to find a permanent cure for diabetes.

Joslin Diabetes Center
One Joslin Place
Boston, MA 02215
(617) 732-2440

Description: Sponsors two camps for diabetic children; maintains an inpatient diabetes treatment unit; provides support groups for parents and children; publishes a series of books on diabetes, including several designed for children.

Juvenile Diabetes Foundation International
432 Park Avenue South
New York, NY 10016
(212) 889-7575

Description: Membership composed of juvenile diabetics and their families; provides counseling and support services to juvenile diabetics and families and strives to educate the public.
Contact: Gloria Pennington, Executive Director

DIGESTIVE DISORDERS

Crohn's & Colitis Foundation of America
444 Park Avenue, South
11th Floor
New York, NY 10016
(800) 343-3637
(212) 685-3440 within New York

Description: Supports research and education, medical symposia, and self-help groups for individuals with inflammatory bowel disease.

• • • • • • • • • • • • • • • • •

HEAD INJURIES

A Chance to Grow
5034 Oliver Avenue, North
Minneapolis, MN 55430
(612) 521-2266

Description: Provides support and information to parents of brain-injured children; also provides counseling, educational material, and other forms of assistance.

The National Head Injury Foundation
1140 Connecticut Avenue, N.W.
Suite 812
Washington, DC 20036
(202) 296-NHIF
(800) 444-NHIF Family Helpline

Description: Serves as a clearinghouse for information and resources related to head injury. Offers 44 state chapters and more than 350 support groups nationwide. Publishes literature on head injuries, including: *Effects of Major and Minor Head Injury in Children; Minor Head Injury in Children — Out of Sight But Not Out of Mind; and Catalogue of Educational Materials.*

HEART DISORDERS

National Center of the American Heart Association
7320 Greenville Avenue
Dallas, TX 75231
(214) 706-1179

Description: Publishes and distributes free pamphlets on various types of heart disease. Also offers educational pamphlets on diet and exercise for children.

KIDNEY DISORDERS

American Kidney Fund
6110 Executive Boulevard
Suite 1010
Rockville, MD 20852
(800) 638-8299

Description: Provides direct financial assistance to needy individuals with kidney disease. Also publishes brochures and makes slide/tape presentations.

National Kidney Foundation
30 East 33rd Street
New York, NY 10016
(800) 622-9010
(212) 889-2210

Description: Provides patient and community services; offers public and professional education; and supports research for the prevention, treatment and cure of kidney/urologic disease.

ASSOCIATIONS

. . . .

LIVER DISORDERS

American Liver Foundation
1425 Pompton Avenue
Suite 1-3
Cedar Grove, NJ 07009
(201) 256-2550

Description: Promotes research, education and patient self-help groups for individuals with liver diseases.

Children's Liver Foundation
14245 Ventura Boulevard
Suite 201
Sherman Oaks, CA 91423
(818) 906-3021

Description: Provides information and advice on treatment centers to parents of children with liver disorders.

LUNG DISORDERS

American Lung Association
1740 Broadway
New York, NY 10019
(212) 315-8700

Description: Provides information about the prevention and control of lung disease.

National Jewish Center for Immunology and Respiratory Medicine
Lung Line
1400 Jackson Street
Denver, CO 80206
(800) 222-LUNG
(303) 355-LUNG within
Denver metropolitan area

Description: Uses trained nurses to answer questions about the detection and management of such lung-related problems as asthma, emphysema, chronic bronchitis, tuberculosis, juvenile rheumatoid arthritis, and allergies.

NEUROLOGICAL DISEASES

Epilepsy Concern Service Group
1282 Wynnewood Drive
West Palm Beach, FL 33417
(407) 683-0044

Description: Starts and maintains self-help groups of epileptics and concerned friends and relatives.
Contact: George L. McKay, Executive Director

• • • • • • • • • • • • • • • • • •

Epilepsy Foundation of America
4351 Garden City Drive
Landover, MD 20785
(800) 332-1000
(301) 459-3700

Description: Distributes educational material. Local organizations provide assistance and counseling.
Contact: William McLin, Executive Vice President

National Multiple Sclerosis Society
205 E. 42nd Street
New York, NY 10017
(800) 624-8236
(212) 986-3240

Description: Provides services and assistance to individuals with MS. Offers on-line computer search services for biomedical databases. Provides 24-hour tape message with information about resources.
Contact: Thor Hansen, President and CEO

The Orton Dyslexia Society
Chester Building, Suite 382
8600 LaSalle Road
Baltimore, MD 21204-6020
(800) 222-2123
(800) ABCD-123
(301) 296-0232

Description: Distributes an information package on detecting and managing dyslexia ($3.00).

United Cerebral Palsy Association
7 Penn Plaza, Suite 804
New York, NY 10001
(800) USA-1UCP
(212) 268-6655

Description: Provides information about prevention and management of cerebral palsy. Distributes free booklets, including Do's and Don'ts for Prospective Mothers and Cerebral Palsy: Facts and Figures.
Contact: John D. Kemp, Executive Director

ORGAN TRANSPLANTS

Children's Transplant Association (CTA)
P.O. Box 53699
Dallas, TX 75253
(214) 287-8484

Description: Provides financial assistance to families of children needing organ transplants. This may include purchase of airline tickets for medical evaluations, emergency air transportation at time of transplant, and funding for lodging, food, and other necessities. CTA will intervene on the patient's behalf to secure funding from private insurance companies and state medicaid programs. CTA owns residence facilities at two major transplant centers and is building others.
Contact: Bettie Bradberry, Executive Director

ASSOCIATIONS

• • • • • • • • • • • • • • • • • • •

Organ Donors
P.O. Box 6725
Houston, TX 77265
(800) 528-2971
(713) 961-9431

Description: Operates the Living Bank, a national organ and tissue donor registry; provides information to individuals interested in donating organs at time of death.

United Network for Organ Sharing
1100 Boulders Parkway
Richmond, VA 23225
(804) 330-8500

Description: Serves as clearinghouse for organs used in U.S. transplant operations. Operates the Organ Center, which matches donated organs with recipients and arranges for transport of organs.

RARE DISORDERS

Cornelia De Lange Syndrome Foundation
c/o Julie Mairano
60 Dyer Avenue
Collinsville, CT 06022
(800) 223-8355
(203) 693-0159

Description: Provides members with medical updates on research into cause and treatment of this rare birth defect.

International Rett Syndrome Association
8511 Rose Marie Drive
Ft. Washington, MD 20744
(301) 248-7031

Description: Distributes brochure, *What Is Rett Syndrome?* Offers parent support; provides accurate and objective information.

National Hydrocephalus Foundation
22427 S. River Road
Joliet, IL 60436
(815) 467-6548 after 4:00 p.m.

Description: Publishes and distributes literature on the specific problems faced by parents of children with hydrocephalus. Moving soon to new office in Wrigley Building, in Chicago. Check for new address and phone number.

National Organization for Rare Disorders
P.O. Box 8923
New Fairfield, CT 06812-1783
(800) 999-6673

Description: Provides assistance to individuals with rare disabilities/illnesses.

• • • • • • • • • • • • • • • • • •

Scleroderma Foundation
1725 York Avenue
Suite 29F
New York, NY 10128
(212) 427-7040

Description: Provides outreach services, educational materials, a helpline, and access to local support groups.

Williams Syndrome Association
1611 Clayton Spur Court
Divide, MO 63011
(314) 227-4411

Description: Offers support and assistance to families with Williams syndrome children.

REYE'S SYNDROME

National Reye's Syndrome Foundation
P.O. Box 829
426 North Lewis
Bryan, OH 43506
(800) 233-7393
(800) 231-7393 within Ohio

Description: Responds to questions about Reye's syndrome; distributes literature; provides referrals to local organizations. Dedicated to informing and educating the public, supporting research, and providing services to individuals with Reye's syndrome.

SCOLIOSIS

Scoliosis Association
P.O. Box 51353
Raleigh, NC 27609-1353
(919) 846-2639

Description: Encourages spinal screening programs in schools; maintains bibliography of scoliosis citations, literature and posters; offers self-help groups for patients and their families.

SPINAL CORD INJURIES

American Paralysis Association
500 Morris Avenue
Springfield, NJ 07081
(800) 526-3456 Spinal Cord Injury Hotline
(800) 225-0292 within New Jersey

Description: Provides referral service hotline for the spinal cord injured and their families.

ASSOCIATIONS

• • • • • • • • • • • • • • • • • • • •

**National Spinal Cord
Injury Association**
600 West Cummings Park
Suite 2000
Woburn, MA 01801
(800) 962-9629

Description: Provides information, referrals, support, and (through local chapters nationwide) prevention programs.

WISH FULFILLMENT ORGANIZATIONS

The Brass Ring Society
314 Main Street
Ottawa, KS 66067
(800) 666-WISH
(913) 242-1666

Description: Offers a variety of programs for children with life-threatening illnesses nationwide. Grants wishes; provides books, equipment and hospital needs and services.

**Children's Wish Foundation
International**
8215 Roswell Road
Building 200
Suite 100
Atlanta, GA 30350
(800) 323-9474

Description: Grants wishes to terminally ill children.
Restrictions: Limited to children under 18 years of age

Dream Factory
P.O. Box 3942
Louisville, KY 40201-3942
(800) 456-7556

Description: Grants wishes to seriously ill children. Sponsors annual summer camp.

Dreams Come True
8184 Baymeadows Way West
Jacksonville, FL 32256
(904) 733-1010

Description: Grants wishes to children with life-threatening illnesses.
Restrictions: Limited to children under 18 years of age who are referred by their physicians and who are receiving treatment in the Jacksonville, Florida area

Famous Fone Friends
9101 Sawyer Street
Los Angeles, CA 90035
(213) 204-5683

Description: Arranges for celebrity actors and athletes to call sick children for cheerful chats. Request must be made by child's physician or nurse.

The Grant-A-Wish Foundation
P.O. Box 21211
Baltimore, MD 21228
(800) 933-5470
(301) 242-1549

Description: Provides services designed to ease the experience of long hospital stays and painful treatment. Grants individual wishes; provides seashore and mountain retreats; offers in-hospital entertainment programs. Manages the Children's House at Johns Hopkins Hospital.

High Hopes Foundation of New Hampshire
P.O. Box 172
North Salem, NH 03073
(603) 898-5333

Description: Grants individual wishes to seriously ill children.
Restrictions: Limited to residents of New Hampshire, ages 18 or younger

Make-A-Wish Foundation of America
2600 N. Central Avenue
Suite 936
Phoenix, AZ 85004
(602) 240-6600

Description: Grants wishes to children suffering from life-threatening illnesses who are not likely to survive beyond their 18th birthdays.
Restrictions: Limited to children ages 2-1/2 to 18

National Alliance of Wish Granting Organizations
3200 Wayne
Suite 106
Kansas City, MO 64109
(800) 666-WISH

Description: Publishes a directory of member wish granting organizations; offers speakers' bureau.

Operation Liftoff
1171 Kings Avenue
Ben Salem, PA 19020
(215) 639-1586
(816) 454-5557 in Kansas
(504) 431-7451 in Louisiana
(207) 848-3157 in Maine
(314) 867-5961 in Missouri
(614) 245-9535 in Ohio
(715) 684-3181 in Wisconsin

Description: Grants wishes to terminally ill children

ASSOCIATIONS

. . . .

Special Love, Inc.
Camp Fantastic
P.O. Box 3243
Winchester, VA 22601
(703) 667-3774

Description: Provides programs/camp for children with cancer

Starlight Foundation
10920 Wilshire Boulevard
Suite 1640
Los Angeles, CA 90024
(800) 274-7827
(213) 208-5885

Description: Arranges and finances trips for chronically, critically and terminally ill children. Also grants other wishes.
Restrictions: Limited to children ages 4 to 18

Sunshine Foundation
4010 Levick Street
Philadelphia, PA 19135
(800) 767-1976
(215) 335-2622

Description: Grants wishes to terminally and chronically ill children whose illnesses have placed their parents under financial strain.

A Wish With Wings
P.O. Box 3457
Arlington, TX 76010
(817) 469-9474
(708) 246-2723

Description: Grants wishes (toys, trips, introductions to celebrities, etc.) to children with life-threatening illnesses.
Restrictions: Limited to children ages 3 to 16

SPECIAL HEALTH CARE FACILITIES

ALSAC - St. Jude Children's Research Hospital
332 N. Lauderdale
Memphis, TN 38101
(901) 522-0300

Description: Treats children without charge. Conducts research on children's catastrophic diseases. Founded by television star Danny Thomas.
Restrictions: Open to children of all races and creeds; admission by physician referral only; limited primarily to children with cancer
Contact: Baddia J. Rashid, Executive Director

. . . .

Children's Hospice International
901 N. Washington St., Ste.. 700
Alexandria, VA 22314
(800) 24-CHILD
(703) 684-0330

Description: Promotes hospice support in pediatric facilities. Distributes literature and videotapes.
Contact: Ann Armstrong Dailey, Founding Director

The Children's House at Johns Hopkins Hospital
The Grant-A-Wish Foundation
P.O. Box 21211
Baltimore, MD 21228
(800) 933-5470
(301) 242-1549

Description: Provides homelike accommodations (18 units) for families and outpatient children receiving treatment at the Johns Hopkins Children's Center. Serves as headquarters for the hospital's pediatric support groups.

City of Hope
1500 East Duarte Road
Duarte, CA 91010
(800) 423-7119

Description: Provides medical care and second opinions to individuals with cancer, leukemia, heart disease, blood disorders, and lung disease. Also performs research.

Johns Hopkins Children's Center
600 N. Wolfe Street
Baltimore, MD 21205
(301) 955-2000

Description: Provides specialized medical care in more than 40 pediatric medical divisions. Offers comprehensive Child Life program, which includes play and school activities, live closed-circuit television programs, and outdoor play areas for inpatients. Provides overnight accommodations for parents.

Little City for Retarded Children
4801 West Peterson
Chicago, IL 60646
(312) 282-2207

Description: Provides services (residential, educational, vocational, recreational, and health and wellness) to individuals with mental retardation and other developmental challenges.

National Institutes of Health
Warren Grant Magnuson
Clinical Center
Building 10, Room 2C146
Bethesda, MD 20892
(301) 496-4891 Clinical
Center's Patient Referral
Services Unit

Description: Provides free medical care to patients participating in NIH studies. Call the patient referral number above for information about illnesses currently being studied and for admission information.
Contact: Director of the Clinical Center, NIH

ASSOCIATIONS

• • • • • • • • • • • • • • • • • • • •

National Jewish Center for Immunology and Respiratory Medicine
1400 Jackson Street
Denver, CO 80206
(800) 222-LUNG

Description: Provides care, treatment and rehabilitation (on an international level) for children with intractable asthma.

Shriner's Hospital for Children
(800) 237-5055
(800) 282-9161 within Florida

Description: Provides free care for children who need orthopaedic or burn treatment. Makes telephone referrals to its 22 hospitals for this care. Call for referral, application and information.

SUPPORT FOR FAMILIES EXPERIENCING THE DEATH OF A CHILD

The Compassionate Friends
P.O. Box 3696
Oak Brook, IL 60522-3696
(708) 990-0010

Description: Directs callers to its 634 local chapters of self-help support groups. Distributes literature and other resources.

ASSOCIATIONS & SERVICES FOR CHILDREN WITH DISABILITIES

GENERAL DISABILITIES

The Association for Persons with Severe Handicaps
7010 Roosevelt Way, N.E.
Seattle, WA 98115
(206) 523-8446

Description: Publishes a monthly newsletter and quarterly journal reporting innovations and research for persons with severe handicaps. Also makes referrals.

Center for Persons with Disabilities
University Medical Center
Utah State University
Logan, UT 84322-6800
(801) 750-1981

Description: Provides direct-service programs for disabled clients of all ages. Works to improve the quality of services provided to persons with disabilities, as well as to improve the quality of life for those persons and their families.

• • • • • • • • • • • • • • • • • • •

Center for Special Education Technology
CEC
1920 Association Drive
Reston, VA 22091
(800) 873-8255
(703) 620-3660

Description: Provides information on using modern technology for children with disabilities.

Child Life Program
Loma Linda University
Medical Center
11234 Anderson Street
Loma Linda, CA 92354
(714) 824-0800 ext. 6555

Description: Assists children with physical handicaps in their reintegration into the school system; provides personnel to visit the school and train staff and teachers to deal with the child's specific needs. Provides information on how to set up similar programs in other areas.

Clearinghouse for Disability Information
330 C Street, S.W.
Washington, DC 20202-2524
(202) 732-1245

Description: Answers questions about children with disabilities. Provides referrals to local organizations. Responds to wide range of inquiries; focus on federally-funded programs serving disabled persons and on federal legislation affecting the disabled community. Provides a publication, *Pocket Guide to Federal Help for Individuals with Disabilities*, upon request.

Cleft Palate Foundation
1218 Grandview Avenue
Pittsburgh, PA 15211
(800) 24-CLEFT

Description: Operates a hotline for parents with children born with cleft lip, cleft palate, or other craniofacial birth defects. Offers free information and quarterly newsletter. Makes referrals to appropriate health care facilities and support groups.

March of Dimes Birth Defects Foundation
National Headquarters
1275 Mamaroneck Avenue
White Plains, NY 10605
(914) 997-4636

Description: Supplies films, exhibits and educational material on birth defects.

National Easter Seal Society, Inc.
70 Eastlake Street
Chicago, IL 60601
(312) 726-6200 Monday–
Friday, 8:30a.m.–5p.m.
Central Standard Time

Description: Provides information on available services, research and technological assistance, as well as referrals.

ASSOCIATIONS

• • • • • • • • • • • • • • • • • • • •

National Foundation of Dentistry for the Handicapped
1600 Stout Street
Denver, CO 80202
(303) 573-0264

Description: Sponsors Campaign of Concern, which helps developmentally disabled persons enjoy good dental health (campaign serves 35,000 people in seven states); offers a referral service; operates Donated Dental Services Program.
Contact: Larry Coffee, D.D.S., Executive Director

National Information for Children and Youth with Disabilities
P.O. Box 1492
Washington, DC 20013
(800) 999-5599
(703) 893-6061
(703) 893-8614 TDD

Description: Answers specific questions. Provides referrals to local organizations. Distributes free literature describing various disabilities and educational options.

Special Clothes for Special Children
P.O. Box 4220
Alexandria, VA 22303
(703) 683-7343

Description: Sells special clothing for children with handicaps; sizes toddler to young adult, pants to jackets to hats. Can custom-design clothes for special problems. Ask for a catalog.

Special Needs Project
1482 E. Valley Road
Suite A121
Santa Barbara, CA 93108
(800) 333-6867 for orders
(805) 565-1914

Description: Offers books about physical and mental disabilities in children. Ask for free catalog.

Toys for Special Children, Inc.
c/o Steven Kanor, Ph.D.
385 Warburton Avenue
Hastings-on-Hudson, NY 10706
(914) 478-0960

Description: Adapts toys with special switches. Toy catalog available for $3.00. Video catalog showing special devices and switches available for $6.50.

ASSOCIATIONS

• • • • • • • • • • • • • • • • • •

BLINDNESS & VISUAL IMPAIRMENT

**American Foundation
for the Blind**
15 W. 16th Street
New York, NY 10011
(800) AF-BLIND
(800) 232-5463
(212) 620-2147 within New York

Description: Serves as a clearinghouse for local and regional agencies for the blind. Operates a hotline answering queries and supplying information on visual impairment. Offers catalog containing such items as Braille Monopoly. Publishes pamphlets, including *Parenting Preschoolers; Suggestions for Raising Young Blind and Visually Impaired Children;* and *Touch the Baby.*

**American Foundation
for the Blind**
Consumer Products Division
15 W. 16th Street
New York, NY 10011
(212) 620-2171
(212) 620-2172

Description: Publishes a catalog of items designed to help blind children (Braille games, watches, etc.). Offers brochures such as *Products for People with Vision Problems* and *What Do You Do When You See a Blind Person?* Also provides information.

Blind Children's Center
4120 Marathon Street
P.O. Box 29159-0159
Los Angeles, CA 90029
(213) 664-2153

Description: Offers free educational correspondence course to families with visually impaired preschool children, with the goal of teaching the parents to facilitate the children's development in several areas.

Blind Children's Fund
230 Central Street
Auburndale, MA 02166
(617) 332-4014

Description: Organization of parents and teachers of visually handicapped children from birth to age seven; promotes the health, education, and welfare of preschool blind and visually impaired infants and young children.
Contact: Sherry Raynor, President

Cornerstone Books
Division of ABC-CLIO
130 Cremona, Box 1911
Santa Barbara, CA 93116-1911
(800) 422-2546

Description: Produces large-print books for children ages 8-15 with impaired vision. Offers large-print Read Alongs for students with special needs.

**Eye Bank for Sight
Restoration**
210 East 64th Street
New York, NY 10021
(212) 980-6700

Description: Collects and distributes healthy corneal tissue

ASSOCIATIONS

• •

Grey Castle Press
Pocket Knife Square
Lakeville, CT 06039
(203) 435-2518
FAX (203) 435-8093

Description: Produces large-print books for young people with impaired vision. Featured are the Nancy Drew, Hardy Boys, and Choose Your Own Adventure series.

Guidedog Foundation for the Blind, Inc.
371 E. Jericho Turnpike
Smithtown, NY 11787
(800) 548-4337
(516) 265-2121

Description: Provides free rehabilitation services through guide dogs and residential training.
Contact: Wells B. Jones, CAE, Executive Director

Helen Keller National Center for Deaf-Blind Youths and Adults
111 Middle Neck Road
Sands Point, NY 11050
(516) 944-8900 Voice/TDD

Description: Serves as a national resource center, providing diagnostic evaluation, short-term comprehensive rehabilitation, and job preparation and placement for deaf/blind Americans nationwide. Offers *Directory of Agencies Serving the Deaf-Blind* ($15.00). Conducts field services through regional offices.
Contact: Stephen S. Barrett, Director

National Association for Parents of the Visually Impaired
2180 Linway Drive
Beloit, WI 53511
(800) 562-6265

Description: Provides support, information and services to parents of visually-impaired children. Publishes *Awareness*, a quarterly newsletter.
Contact: Eileen Hudson, President

National Association for the Visually Handicapped
East Coast Address
22 West 21st Street
New York, NY 10010
(212) 889-3141
West Coast Address
(for the 13 western states, plus Alaska and Hawaii)
3201 Balboa Street
San Francisco, CA 94121
(415) 221-8753

Description: Distributes information, large-print materials and visual aids. Offers referrals, as well as public and professional education programs.

National Society to Prevent Blindness
500 East Remington Road
Schaumburg, IL 60173
(800) 221-3004

Description: Produces free publications focusing on prevention, such as the *Family Home Eye Test* and *Your Child's Sight*. Advocates industrial and sports safety.

Recording for the Blind
20 Roszel Road
Princeton, NJ 08540
(609) 452-0606

Description: Provides free educational books to blind and visually-impaired individuals.

DEAFNESS & HEARING IMPAIRMENT

Alexander Graham Bell Association for the Deaf
Parents Section
Information Services
3417 Volta Place, N.W.
Washington, DC 20007
(202) 337-5220

Description: Offers publications on the problems of deaf and hearing-impaired children. Emphasis on the educational, social and psychological needs of these children. Sponsors financial aid programs for profoundly hearing-impaired oral children, infants through college age.
Contact: Donna McCord Dickman, Ph. D., Executive Director

American Society for Deaf Children
814 Thayer Avenue
Silver Spring, MD 20910
(301) 585-5400 Voice/TDD

Description: Provides information and encouragement to families with deaf children.

Assessment Center for Hearing-Impaired Children and Youth
Kendall Demonstration Elementary School
Gallaudet University
800 Florida Avenue, N.E.
Washington, DC 20002
(202) 651-5337
(202) 651-5031 Voice/TDD

Description: Serves as model diagnostic program, disseminating methods, materials and research findings related to hearing-impairment assessment.
Contact: Jean Moore, Coordinator

ASSOCIATIONS

• • • • • • • • • • • • • • • • • • • •

Deafpride, Inc.
1350 Potomac Avenue, S.E.
Washington, DC 20003
(202) 675-6700 Voice/TTY

Description: Offers a variety of programs, including Project Access, which helps deaf women and families ensure their access to health care; and Project AIDS, which provides AIDS education to the deaf community and ensures access to AIDS treatment programs.

Deaf-Reach
3722 12th Street, N.E.
Washington, DC 20017
(202) 832-6681

Description: Promotes the establishment of residential homes and provides aid to deaf persons with mental and emotional problems.
Contact: Carole Schauer, Executive Director

Dogs for the Deaf
10175 Wheeler Road
Central Point, OR 97502
(503) 826-9220

Descripton: Provides hearing ear dogs to deaf persons to alert them to certain sounds; costs of dog selection, veterinary care, housing, training, and placement are covered by the association.
Contact: Robin Dickson, Executive Director

Hear Center
301 East Del Mar Boulevard
Pasadena, CA 91101
(213) 681-4641

Description: Program to help hearing-impaired children, infants, and adults; provides services such as diagnosis, speech therapy, and parent counseling.
Contact: Josephine F. Wilson, Executive Director

Helen Keller National Center for Deaf-Blind Youths and Adults
111 Middle Neck Road
Sands Point, NY 11050
(516) 944-8900 Voice/TDD

Description: Serves as a national resource center, providing diagnostic evaluation, short-term comprehensive rehabilitation, and job preparation and placement for deaf/blind Americans nationwide. Offers *Directory of Agencies Serving the Deaf-Blind* ($15.00). Conducts field services through regional offices.
Contact: Stephen S. Barrett, Director

International Hearing Dogs, Inc.
5901 E. 89th Avenue
Henderson, CO 80640
(303) 287-3277

Description: Trains and places dogs with deaf or hearing-impaired individuals living independently. Also places dogs with individuals who have multiple handicaps. No charge.
Restrictions: Limited to individuals with 65-decibel loss, living alone or with other hearing-impaired persons, who have no other dog, and are mentally and physically capable of handling a dog.
Contact: Martha A. Foss, President

National Captioning Institute
5203 Leesburg Pike
Falls Church, VA 22041
(703) 998-2400 Voice/TTY

Description: Provides captioning for the hearing impaired; useful for children with learning disabilities and for individuals studying English as a second language.

National Institutes of Health
Consumer Information Center
Department 573X
Pueblo, CO 81009

Description: Offers free publication, U.S. *Government* TDD *Directory* (573X), listing federal agencies that have telecommunications devices for the deaf, and explaining how to reach hearing- or speech-impaired federal employees if you do not use a TDD.

Registry of Interpreters for the Deaf, Inc.
8719 Colesville Road
Suite 310
Silver Spring, MD 20910
(301) 608-0050 Voice/TTY

Description: Maintains a registry of certified interpreters for the deaf. Publishes books and other literature relating to the profession of interpreting for the deaf.

TRIPOD Grapevine
2901 N. Keystone Street
Burbank, CA 91504
(800) 352-8888
(800) 2-TRIPOD within California

Description: Answers specific questions about educating, rearing and living with a hearing-impaired child, using its worldwide advisory board as a resource. Provides referrals. Loans to parents, upon request, two open-captioned videotapes: *Language Says It All* and *Once Upon A Time*.

SPEECH & LANGUAGE DISORDERS

National Center for Stuttering
200 E. 33 Street
New York, NY 10016
(800) 221-2483
(212) 532-1460

Description: Distributes free information on stuttering treatment programs nationwide.

National Council on Stuttering
Box 40742
Indianapolis, IN 46240-0742

Description: Offers literature on stuttering, self-help groups, and referrals to local organizations.

ASSOCIATIONS

. . . .

National Institutes
of Health
Consumer Information Center
Department 448X
Pueblo, CO 81009

Description: Offers a booklet, *Development Speech and Language Disorders* (448X), for 50¢; it addresses types of speech/language problems children may have and includes a chart of language milestones for ages 1 to 6.

National Stuttering Project
4601 Irving Street
San Francisco, CA 94122-1020
(415) 566-5324

Description: Offers literature on stuttering, self-help groups, and referrals to local organizations.
Contact: John Ahlbach, Executive Director

Speak Easy International
Foundation
233 Concord Drive
Paramus, NJ 07652
(201) 262-0895

Description: Offers literature on stuttering, self-help groups, and referrals to local organizations.

MENTAL HEALTH ASSOCIATIONS & SERVICES

GENERAL MENTAL HEALTH

Anxiety Disorders
Association of America
6000 Executive Boulevard
Rockville, MD 20852
(301) 231-9350

Description: Serves as a clearinghouse for resources and self-help groups that treat anxiety disorders.

Children with Attention-
Deficit Disorders
499 N.W. 70th Avenue
Suite 308
Plantation, FL 33317
(305) 587-3700

Description: Provides parents and teachers with support and educational material for dealing with attention-deficit disorders.

Creative Therapeutics
P.O. Box R
Cresskill, NJ 07626
(800) 544-6162
(201) 567-7295

Description: Publishes a catalog of literature available to help children cope with such emotionally demanding experiences as divorce, illness and adoption.

• • • • • • • • • • • • • • • • • •

National Alliance for the Mentally Ill
Children and Adolescents Network
2101 Wilson Blvd., Suite 302
Arlington, VA 22201
(703) 524-7600

Description: Provides support, information and advocacy for parents of mentally ill and/or emotionally disturbed children.

National Foundation for Depressive Illness
(800) 248-4344

Description: Provides a recorded message describing the symptoms of clinical depression and giving an address for more information and physician referral.

National Institute of Mental Health
Consumer Information Center
Department 541X
Pueblo, CO 81009

Description: Distributes a free publication, A *Consumer's Guide to Mental Health Services* (541X), which addresses common questions about mental health and its treatment.

National Institute of Mental Health
Consumer Information Center
Department 546X
Pueblo, CO 81009

Description: Distributes a free publication, *Schizophrenia: Questions and Answers* (546X), which describes the causes, treatments and outlook for schizophrenia.

National Institute of Mental Health
Information Resources and Inquiries Branch
5600 Fishers Lane, Rm. 15C-05
Rockville, MD 20857
(301) 443-4513
(301) 443-4514

Description: Distributes the following publications on child mental health: *Plain Talk About Dealing with the Angry Child* (ADM 79-781); *Plain Talk About Raising Children* (ADM 79-875); and *Plain Talk About When Your Child Starts School* (ADM 80-1021).

Phobia Society of America
Department H
P.O. Box 42514
Washington, DC 20015-05141

Description: Publishes a free booklet, *Phobic & Panic Disorders: Getting Help.*

ASSOCIATIONS

• • • • • • • • • • • • • • • • • • • •

Wisconsin Clearinghouse
University of Wisconsin
P.O. Box 1468
Madison, WI 53701-1468
(800) 322-1468
(608) 263-2797

Description: Publishes a booklet, *Adolescence and Depression*, which is available upon request for $1.00. Also provides a free catalog of hundreds of resources on alcohol/drug abuse and mental health.

EATING DISORDERS

American Anorexia/Bulimia Association
418 E. 76th Street
New York, NY 10021
(212) 734-1114

Description: Serves as an information and referral service for people dealing with anorexia and bulimia.

BASH
6125 Clayton Ave., Suite 215
St. Louis, MO 63139
(314) 768-3292 Crisis
Hotline; 24 hours a day
(800) 768-3838
within Missouri
(800) 227-4785
BASH Information;
Monday–Friday, 9a.m.–5p.m.

Description: Offers a 24-hour crisis-intervention hotline. Provides free literature on bulimia and anorexia. Not a referral service.

National Association of Anorexia Nervosa and Associated Disorders
P.O. Box 7
Highland Park, IL 60035
(708) 831-3438

Description: Provides children's services, offers a referral service, and maintains a speakers' bureau.

Office of Research Reporting
National Institute of Child
Health & Human Development
Building 31, Room 2A-32
National Institutes of Health
9000 Rockville Pike
Bethesda, MD 20892
(301) 496-5133

Description: Distributes a free publication, *Obesity in Childhood*, which describes approaches for solving the problem of childhood obesity.

Overeaters Anonymous, Inc.
4025 Spencer Street
Suite 203
Torrance, CA 90503
(213) 618-8835

Description: Offers free membership and mutual support to those who want to stop eating compulsively.

MENTAL RETARDATION

American Association on Mental Retardation
1719 Kalorama Road, N.W.
Washington, DC 20009
(202) 387-1968

Description: Provides information on the cause, treatment and prevention of mental retardation. Promotes quality professional services.

Association for Retarded Citizens
500 E. Border Street
3rd Floor
Arlington, TX 76010
(817) 261-6003

Description: Provides referrals to appropriate local organizations.

Learning Disabilities Association of America
4156 Library Road
Pittsburgh, PA 15234
(412) 341-1515

Description: Serves as a clearinghouse for problems associated with children's learning disabilities. Distributes publications on the subject.

Private Foundation Funding

The listings in this chapter are probably the easiest and most accessible funding sources for the average individual seeking a grant. Until now, this information has not been readily available to the general public. And yet thousands of foundations give away millions of dollars to individuals to help them pay for medical treatment and other needs associated with injury and illness. Much of this money is specifically earmarked for the health care needs of children.

Do you just walk up, hold out your hand, and expect someone to put money in it? Of course not. Getting grant money takes time, effort and thought on your part. You are going to have to find out who is giving away money. You are going to have to fill out applications. You may meet with frustration or rejection somewhere down the road. The odds, however, are in your favor that you will qualify for some sort of funding.

The information in this chapter is organized by state. Wherever possible, each listing includes a description of what the foundation funds, any restrictions (i.e., you must reside in a particular town or county), the total amount of money awarded annually, the number of grants or loans made annually, the range of monies given, the average size of the award, information on how to apply, deadline date(s), and name(s) of contact person(s).

PRIVATE FOUNDATION FUNDING

• •

ALABAMA

Kate Kinloch Middleton Fund
P.O. Drawer 2527
Mobile, AL 36601

Description: Grants or low interest loans to help defray the costs of unexpected serious illness
Restrictions: Limited to residents of Mobile County, Alabama
$ Given: In FY89, 63 grants totaling $108,286 were awarded to individuals; range, $135 - $8,094
Application Information: Initial approach by interview
Deadline: N/A
Contact: Joan Sapp

CALIFORNIA

Avery-Fuller Children's Center
251 Kearney Street
Number 301
San Francisco, CA 94108
(415) 930-8292
(415) 986-1687

Description: Grants to handicapped and disabled children for physical therapy, medical services, special schools, psychotherapy, prescriptions, appliances, and related services.
Restrictions: Both patient and primary care professional must be residents of San Francisco, San Mateo, Marin, Alameda, or Contra Costa counties, California
$ Given: FY1989, grants totaling $151,667 were awarded
Application Information: Initial contact by phone or letter; applications are submitted by primary care professional (social worker, teacher, therapist, or physician)
Deadlines: February 14, May 14, August 14, and November 14
Contact: Bonnie Van Manen Pinkel, Executive Director

William Babcock Memorial Endowment
305 San Anselmo Avenue
Suite 219
San Anselmo, CA 94960
(415) 453-0901

Description: Grants and loans to persons burdened with exceptional medical expenses which exceed insurance coverage and fall outside the purview of other community agencies
Restrictions: Limited to persons who have been residents of Marin County, California, for two or more years
$ Given: In FY89, 480 grants totaling $455,170 were awarded to individuals; range, $50 - $$10,000
Application Information: Call for application guidelines; formal application required
Deadline: None
Contact: Executive Director

• • • • • • • • • • • • • • • • • • • •

Albert B. Cutter
Memorial Fund
Security Pacific National Bank
Trust Department
P.O. Box 712
Riverside, CA 92501
(714) 781-1523
ADDITIONAL ADDRESS:
P.O. Box 3189
Terminal Annex
Los Angeles, CA 92501

Description: Limited grants to persons in extreme circumstances who are not eligible for other sources of aid.
Restrictions: Applicants must have been permanent residents of Riverside County, California for at least one year, and must have been referred by a local agency
$ Given: In 1989, 26 grants totaling $6,650 were awarded to individuals; range, $22 - $550
Application Information: Applications are accepted from local agencies; individuals are referred by these agencies; formal application required; interview or presentation required
Deadline: None
Contact: Executive Secretary, Trust Department

Jefferson (John Percival
and Mary C.) Endowment
Fund
114 East De La Guerra
Santa Barbara, CA 93012
(805) 963-8822

Description: Emergency relief assistance for medical, dental, and living expenses
Restrictions: Limited to residents of Santa Barbara County, California
$ Given: In FY89, 30 grants totaling $63,000 were awarded to individuals; range, $100 - $6,500
Application Information: Initial contact by letter; formal application required
Deadline: N/A
Contact: Patricia M. Brouard, Trustee

Cornelia M. Moore Free
Dental Foundation
c/o Wells Fargo Bank
525 Market Street, 17th Fl.
San Francisco, CA 94103

Description: Financial assistance for dental expenses to individuals under 18 years of age; monies paid directly to dentist providing care.
Restrictions: Limited to residents of Santa Barbara, California; grants not to exceed $300 on foundation fee schedule; family must provide $20 co-payment.
$ Given: In 1989, 140 grants totaling $16,660 were awarded to individuals; general range, $35 - $300
Application Information: Formal application required; interviews required
Deadline: None
Contact: Janet Reed Koed, Director, Dental Health Services

PRIVATE FOUNDATION FUNDING

• • • • • • • • • • • • • • • • • • • •

Charles E. Saak Trust
c/o Wells Fargo Bank
Trust Department
2222 West Shaw Avenue
Suite 11
Fresno, CA 93711
(209) 442-6232
(209) 442-6206

Description: One-time grants for dental and emergency medical treatment for children under 21 years of age.
Restrictions: Limited to residents of the Porterville/Poplar area of Tulare County, California
$ Given: FY1989, 140 grants totaling $42,380 were awarded to individuals; range, $50 - $1,375; general range, $300 - $900
Application Information: Formal application required; include purpose and cost estimate statements and parents financial statement (with copy of most recent tax return)
Deadline: March 31
Contact: N/A

COLORADO

Curtis (Effie H. and Edward H.) Trust Fund
c/o United Bank of Fort Collins, N.A.
P.O. Box 2203
Fort Collins, CO 80522
(303) 482-1100

Description: Emergency medical grants for children under 18 years old; monies paid directly to hospitals or other institutions providing care.
Restrictions: Limited to permanent residents of Larimer County, Colorado
$ Given: In 1989, 46 grants totaling $40,000 were awarded to individuals; range, $15 - $3,000
Application Information: Formal application required, including letter from attending physician; include copy of tax return
Deadline: 15th of each month
Contact: Kelly Wiedeman

CONNECTICUT

Blue Horizon Health & Welfare Trust
c/o Reid and Riege
Lakeville, CT 06039
(203) 435-9251

Description: Financial assistance for medical costs
Restrictions: Limited to residents of Connecticut
$ Given: Grant awards range, $25 - $500
Application Information: Initial contact by letter
Deadline: None
Contact: Frances M. Wagner, Trustee

The Westport-Weston Foundation
c/o The Westport Bank & Trust Company
P.O. Box 5177
Westport, CT 06881
(203) 222-6911

Description: Grants for medical and basic living expenses
Restrictions: Limited to residents of Westport and Weston, Connecticut
$ Given: Grants range, $50 - $400
Application Information: Initial contact by letter
Deadline: N/A
Contact: Susanne M. Allen, Trust Officer

DELAWARE

Delaware Foundation-Quigley Trust
P.O. Box 1669
Wilmington, DE 19899

Description: Grants for medication and medical care
Restrictions: Limited to residents of Delaware
$ Given: Grants range, $50 - $1,500
Application Information: Formal application required; request application form from the foundation
Deadline: None
Contact: N/A

FLORIDA

Gore Family Memorial Foundation
501 East Las Olas
Fort Lauderdale, FL 33302

Description: One-time and short-term assistance grants for medical expenses, equipment for the handicapped, and housing and transportation costs.
Restrictions: Limited to residents of Broward County, Florida and surrounding areas
$ Given: In FY89, 390 relief assistance grants totaling $279,250 were awarded to individuals
Application Information: Write for application guidelines
Deadline: None
Contact: N/A

Roy M. Speer Foundation
1803 U.S. Highway 19
Holiday, FL 34691-5536

Description: Grants to individuals in financial difficulty, due to family medical problems.
Restrictions: Limited to residents of Florida
$ Given: In FY88, one grant of $4,000 was awarded
Application Information: Initial approach by letter
Deadline: None
Contact: Richard W. Baker, Trustee

PRIVATE FOUNDATION FUNDING

●　●

GEORGIA

Thomas C. Burke Foundation
182 Riley Avenue
No. B
Macon, GA 31204-2345
(912) 745-1442

Description: Medical assistance in one of three forms: (1) one-time payments for doctor bills, medical equipment and pharmacy bills; (2) weekly grants of up to $60 to assist with medical expenses; or (3) grants for transportation to medical facilities.
Restrictions: Limited to residents of Bibb County, Georgia
$ Given: In FY89, an unspecified number of grants totaling $120,722 were awarded
Application Information: Initial contact by phone
Deadline: None
Contact: Carolyn P. Griggers

HAWAII

The Hawaii Community Foundation
222 Merchant Street
Honolulu, HI 96813
(808) 537-6333

Description: Financial assistance for children with medical and other needs; provided through the Irving L. Singer Funds and the Kitaro Watanabe Fund.
Restrictions: Limited to residents of Hawaii; Singer Funds specify children of Hawaiian ancestry
$ Given: In 1989, 116 grants totaling $78,110 were awarded to individuals; general range, $100 - $1,000
Application Information: Initial contact by phone; formal application required
Deadline: None
Contact: Suzanne Toguchi, Program Officer

IDAHO

Idaho In-Home Financial Assistance Program
Division of Community Rehabilitation
Department of Health and Welfare
Boise, ID 83720

Description: Grants to parents of developmentally disabled children under age 22 for carrying out a planned program of home-based care and training for the children.
Restrictions: Limited to parents residing in Idaho; priority given to parents whose children are institutionalized and will return to their homes, as well as to parents of children for whom institutionalization is imminent
$ Given: Grants of up to $250 per month per child (no grant may exceed 3 percent of the current average institutional cost for the child); funds may not be used for education or educational-related services
Application Information: N/A
Deadline: None
Contact: N/A

• • • • • • • • • • • • • • • • • • •

**Rouch (A.P. and Louise)
Boys Foundation**
c/o Twin Falls Bank &Trust
Trust Department
P.O. Box 7
Twin Falls, ID 83303-0007

Description: Grants for medical care, clothing, and summer camp fees
Restrictions: Limited to residents of the Magic Valley area of Idaho
$ Given: In 1988, 74 grants totaling $9,285 were awarded to individuals; range, $5 - $1,605
Application Information: Initial approach by letter
Deadline: N/A
Contact: N/A

ILLINOIS

Reade Industrial Fund
c/o Harris Trust and Savings
Bank
P.O. Box 755
111 West Monroe Street
Chicago, IL 60690
(312) 461-2609

Description: Emergency loans or grants to individuals who are unable to care for themselves and/or their family members.
Restrictions: Limited to persons who are currently or who have previously been employed in industry in Illinois
$ Given: In 1988, 51 grants totaling $161,900 were awarded to individuals; range, $373 - $5,000
Application Information: Initial contact by letter; formal application required
Deadline: None
Contact: Ronald F. Tuite, Jr.

INDIANA

Mosette Levin Trust
c/o First Citizens Bank, N.A.
Trust Department
P.O. Box 1125
Michigan City, IN 46360
(800) 873-7001

Description: Grants for medical treatment, purchase of medication, or transportation to receive treatment for children under 16 suffering from any childhood illness, and for individuals over 16 suffering from cancer.
Restrictions: Limited to residents of La Porte County, Indiana
$ Given: In 1988, 21 grants totaling $11,120 were awarded; general range, $20 - $1,000
Application Information: Formal application required; interviews required
Deadline: None
Contact: N/A

PRIVATE FOUNDATION FUNDING

• • • • • • • • • • • • • • • • • •

KANSAS

Jones (Walter S. and Evan C.) Foundation
527 Commercial Street
Room 515
Emporia, KS 66801
(316) 342-1714
ADDITIONAL ADDRESS:
c/o Bank IV Emporia
Emporia, KS 66801

Description: Financial assistance for medical expenses; grants based on demonstrated financial need.
Restrictions: Applicants must have been continuous residents of Lyon, Coffey or Osage counties, Kansas, for at least one year; applicants must be under 21 years of age
$ Given: In FY89, 2,192 medical assistance grants totaling $625,074 were awarded to individuals; range, $60 - $6,173
Application Information: Initial contact by letter; formal application required; interviews required; parents of applicant must submit comprehensive financial statement
Deadline: Prior to beginning of medical services
Contact: Sharon R. Brown, General Manager

MAINE

Anita Card Montgomery Foundation
20 Mechanic Street
Camden, ME 04843-1707

Description: Grants to needy individuals, including funding for medical and dental expenses
Restrictions: Limited to residents of Rockport, Camden, Hope, and Lincolnville, Maine
$ Given: In 1988, 16 grants totaling $14,820; range, $40 - $4,060
Application Information: Write for guidelines
Deadline: None
Contact: Robert C. Perkins

Portland Female Charitable Society
20 Noyes Street
Portland, ME 04103
APPLICATION ADDRESS:
142 Pleasant Street
No. 761
Portland, ME 04101

Description: Financial aid for medical and dental expenses for children, as well as for the elderly.
Restrictions: Limited to residents of Portland, Maine
$ Given: In FY89, 33 grants totaling $9,550 were awarded; range, $20 - $850
Application Information: Write for information; applications are usually presented by health care professionals or social workers; interviews required
Deadline: None
Contact: Janet Matty

• • • • • • • • • • • • • • • • • • •

MASSACHUSETTS

The Pilgrim Foundation
478 Torrey Street
Brockton, MA 02401-4654
(508) 586-6100

Description: Financial assistance to families and children
Restrictions: Limited to residents of Brockton, Massachusetts
$ Given: Welfare assistance grants totaling $7,230 awarded to individuals
Application Information: Formal application required
Deadline: N/A
Contact: Executive Director

Shaw Fund for Mariners' Children
c/o Russell Brier & Company
50 Congress Street, Room 800
Boston, MA 02109
APPLICATION ADDRESS:
64 Concord Avenue
Norwood, MA 02062

Description: Grants to financially distressed mariners and their families
Restrictions: Limited to mariners, their wives or widows, and their children; Massachusetts residents only
$ Given: Grants totaling $114,140 awarded to individuals
Application Information: Write for program information
Deadline: None
Contact: Clare M. Tolias

Urann Foundation
P.O. Box 1788
Brockton, MA 02403
(508) 588-7744

Description: Medical assistance grants for Massachusetts families engaged in cranberry farming and processing; grants intended to assist in payment of hospital and medical bills
Restrictions: Limited to families located in Massachusetts
$ Given: In 1989, 22 grants totaling $44,460 were awarded; 1 medical assistance grant for $680 was awarded
Application Information: Initial contact by phone or letter
Deadline: None
Contact: Howard Whelan, Administrator

MICHIGAN

Michigan Veterans Trust Fund for Temporary Emergency Needs
Michigan Veterans Trust Fund
P.O. Box 30026
Ottawa Street Office Building
Lansing, MI 48909

Description: Grants to provide temporary assistance to disabled children of veterans and others facing personal emergencies.
Restrictions: Limited to disabled children of Michigan veterans who served for at least 180 days during wartime or other national emergency; veterans themselves, their widow(er)s, and children under 18 also eligible.
$ Given: Number of grants varies; local boards in each Michigan county determine need and amount
Application Information: N/A
Deadline: None
Contact: N/A

PRIVATE FOUNDATION FUNDING

. . . .

MINNESOTA

Fanny S. Gilfillan Memorial, Inc.
c/o Lawrence Harder, Rte. 4
Redwood Falls, MN 56283
APPLICATION ADDRESS:
Redwood County Welfare
Department, Box 27
Redwood Falls, MN 56283
(507) 637-5741

Description: Grants for medical, dental, and hospitalization costs to those not eligible for aid through county or other sources.
Restrictions: Limited to needy residents of Redwood County, Minnesota
$ Given: In 1988, 50 grants totaling $52,400 were awarede; range, $70 - $5,000
Application Information: Write to request guidelines; formal application and interview required.
Deadline: None
Contact: Lawrence Harder

Charles D. Gilfillan Paxton Memorial, Inc.
c/o Thomas W. Murray,
Vice President
W-555 First National Bank
Building
St. Paul, MN 55101
(612) 291-6236
APPLICATION ADDRESS:
Committee of Beneficiaries
200 First Street Southwest
Rochester, MN 55901
(507) 282-2511

Description: Medical, surgical and dental assistance to Minnesota residents in financial need; priority given to those in rural areas and towns with populations of less than 3,000.
Restrictions: Limited to residents of Minnesota
$ Given: In FY89, 81 grants totaling $39,900 were awarded to individuals; range, $38 - $2,160; average, $500
Application Information: Formal application required
Deadline: None
Contact: Marie LaPlante, Secretary

The Saint Paul Foundation
1120 Norwest Center
St. Paul, MN 55101
(612) 224-5463

Description: Relief assistance grants
Restrictions: Limited to residents of St. Paul and Minneapolis, Minnesota, and to employees of 3M Company
$ Given: 15 relief assistance grants totaling $42,504 awarded to individuals
Application Information: Write or call for guidelines
Deadline: N/A
Contact: Paul A. Verret, President

MISSOURI

Herschend Family Foundation
c/o Jack R. Herschend
Silver Dollar City, Inc.
Branson, MO 65616
(417) 338-2611

Description: Assistance to individuals in need
Restrictions: Intended primarily for residents of Missouri
$ Given: In 1989, 34 grants totaling $250,430 were awarded to individuals
Application Information: Call or write, explaining need
Deadline: None
Contact: Jack R. Herschend, Director

NEW HAMPSHIRE

Abbie M. Griffin Hospital Fund
111 Concord Street
Nashua, NH 03060

Description: Grants for payment of hospital bills
Restrictions: Limited to residents of Merrimack, Hillsborough County, New Hampshire
$ Given: In 1988, 4 grants totaling $11,000 were awarded to individuals; range, $2,221 - $3,370
Application Information: Write for guidelines
Deadline: None
Contact: S. Robert Winer, Trustee

Zaida J. MacFadden Dental Trust
P.O. Box 201
Wolfeboro, NH 03894-0201

Description: Funding for dental care for children
Restrictions: Limited to residents of Wolfeboro, New Hampshire
$ Given: In 1988, grants to individuals totaled $3,600.
Application Information: Formal application required
Deadline: None
Contact: N/A

Ida E. Walton Trust
189 Union Avenue
Laconia, NH 03246
APPLICATION ADDRESS:
c/o Paul L. Normandin,
Trustee
213 Union Avenue
Laconia, NH 03246

Description: Grants for medical care and clothing for financially distressed children
Restrictions: Limited to residents of New Hampshire
$ Given: In 1989, 12 grants totaling $2,026 were awarded; average range, $40 - $500
Application Information: Write stating need
Deadline: N/A
Contact: Paul L. Normandin, Trustee

43

PRIVATE FOUNDATION FUNDING

• •

NEW JERSEY

Otto Sussman Trust
P.O. Box 1374
Trainsmeadow Station
Flushing, NY 11370-9998

Description: Financial assistance for medical bills and care-giving expenses to individuals with serious or terminal illnesses.
Restrictions: Limited to residents of New York, New Jersey, Oklahoma, and Pennsylvania
$ Given: Grants range, $329 - $4,000
Application Information: Write letter requesting application form and guidelines; explain circumstances of need; formal application required
Deadline: None
Contact: Edward S. Miller, Trustee

NEW MEXICO

Walter Hightower Foundation
c/o Texas Commerce Bank-El Paso
P.O. Drawer 140
. El Paso, TX 79980
(915) 546-6515

Description: Funding for medical, dental, and vision treatment, prescriptions, orthopedic devices, and speech therapy to children.
Restrictions: Limited to services provided in west Texas and southern New Mexico
$ Given: In 1988, 657 grants totaling $109,000 were awarded to individuals; range, $10 - $3,600 per award
Application Information: Initial contact by letter; formal application required
Deadline: July 1
Contact: Terry Crenshaw, Charitable Services Officer, Texas CommerceBank-El Paso

NEW YORK

Brockway Foundation for the Needy of the Village and Township of Homer, New York
c/o Key Bank
25 South Main Street
Homer, NY 13077-1314

Description: Financial assistance based on need
Restrictions: Limited to residents of the Homer, New York area
$ Given: Grants range, $180 - $600
Application Information: Write for guidelines
Deadline: None
Contact: M. Lee Swartwout, Treasurer

44

PRIVATE FOUNDATION FUNDING

The Clark Foundation
30 Wall Street
New York, NY 10005
(212) 269-1833

Description: Financial aid for medical and hospital care to needy individuals in upstate New York and New York City.
Restrictions: Limited to residents of upstate New York state
$ Given: In FY89, 18 grants totaling $108,330 were awarded to individuals; range, $560 - $15,600
Application Information: Write for guidelines
Deadline: None
Contact: Edward W. Stack, Secretary

Josiah H. Danforth Memorial Fund
8 Fremont Street
Gloversville, NY 12078

Description: Financial aid for medical care
Restrictions: Limited to residents of Fulton County, New York
$ Given: In 1989, 95 grants totaling $18,610 were awarded to individuals; range, $16 - $500; average, $200; maximum grant per person per year, $500
Application Information: Write for guidelines, application form; formal application required
Deadline: None
Contact: N/A

Saranac Lake Voluntary Health Association, Inc.
70 Main Street
Saranac Lake, NY 12983

Description: Grants for dental treatment for students as well as funding for visiting nurse services for the elderly.
Restrictions: Students must attend school in the Saranac Lake School District
$ Given: In FY89, 3 grants totaling $42,122 were awarded; range, $4,500 - $31,610
Application Information: Write letter describing needs
Deadline: N/A
Contact: N/A

Otto Sussman Trust
P.O. Box 1374
Trainsmeadow Station
Flushing, NY 11370-9998

Description: Financial assistance for medical bills and care-giving expenses to individuals with serious or terminal illnesses.
Restrictions: Limited to residents of New York, New Jersey, Oklahoma, and Pennsylvania
$ Given: Grants range, $329 - $4,000
Application Information: Write letter requesting application form and guidelines; explain circumstances of need; formal application required
Deadline: None
Contact: Edward S. Miller, Trustee

PRIVATE FOUNDATION FUNDING

• •

VonderLinden Charitable Trust
c/o Leonard Rachmilowitz
26 Mill Street
Rhinebeck, NY 12572
(914) 876-3021

Description: Grants for financially distressed residents of upstate New York; funds may be used to meet a variety of needs, including medical bills.
Restrictions: Limited to residents of upstate New York
$ Given: In FY89, 101 grants totaling $23,260 were awarded to individuals; range, $4 - $540
Application Information: Write or call for guidelines
Deadline: None
Contact: Leonard Rachmilowitz

NORTH CAROLINA

Community Foundation of Gaston County, Inc.
(formerly Garrison Community Foundation of Gaston County, Inc.)
P.O. Box 123
Gastonia, NC 28053
(704) 864-0927

Description: Grants for medical expenses only
Restrictions: Limited to children, age 18 and younger, who are residents of Gaston County, North Carolina
$ Given: An unspecified number of grants totaling $9,000 awarded to individuals
Application Information: Write for guidelines and application forms; formal application required; interviews required
Deadline: None
Contact: Harold T. Sumner, Executive Director

OHIO

Columbus Female Benevolent Society
228 South Drexel Avenue
Columbus, OH 43209

Description: Grants for clothing and other infant needs; aid for handicapped infants
Restrictions: Limited to residents of Franklin County, Ohio
$ Given: In 1989, an unspecified number of grants totaling $32,800 were awarded to individuals
Application Information: No direct applications; recipients are referred by people in the community who are familiar with their circumstances
Deadline: N/A
Contact: N/A

James R. Nicholl
Memorial Foundation
c/o The Central Trust
Company of Northern Ohio
Trust Department
1949 Broadway
Lorain, OH 44052
(216) 244-1965

Description: Financial assistance for medical and surgical services to needy children (2 to 21 years of age); grants are paid directly to health care providers.
Restrictions: Limited to children who have been residents of Lorain County, Ohio for at least two years
$ Given: In 1989, 11 medical assistance grants totaling $26,550 were awarded; range $14 - $4,040
Application Information: Write for informational brochure and application guidelines; indicate medical need; formal application required
Deadline: None
Contact: David E. Nocjar, Trust Officer

OKLAHOMA

Otto Sussman Trust
P.O. Box 1374
Trainsmeadow Station
Flushing, NY 11370-9998

Description: Financial assistance for medical bills and caregiving expenses to individuals with serious or terminal illnesses
Restrictions: Limited to residents of New York, New Jersey, Oklahoma, and Pennsylvania
$ Given: Grants range, $329 - $4,000
Application Information: Write letter requesting application form and guidelines; explain circumstances of need; formal application required
Deadline: None
Contact: Edward S. Miller, Trustee

OREGON

The Elizabeth Church
Clarke Testamentary Trust/
Fund Foundation
U.S. National Bank of Oregon
P.O. Box 3168
Portland, OR 97208
(503) 228-9405
APPLICATION ADDRESS:
Scottish Rite Temple
709 S.W. 15th Avenue
Portland, OR 97205

Description: Grants for medical assistance; payments may be made directly to the individuals or to the physicians and hospitals providing services.
Restrictions: Limited to residents of Oregon
$ Given: In 1989, total giving was $32,770
Application Information: Initial contact by letter detailing needs and costs
Deadline: None
Contact: G.L. Selmyhr, Executive Secretary

PRIVATE FOUNDATION FUNDING

• • • • • • • • • • • • • • • • • • •

Blanche Fischer Foundation
1001 South West Fifth
Avenue
Suite 1550
Portland, OR 97204
(503) 323-9111

Description: Financial aid for physically handicapped persons in Oregon
Restrictions: Limited to Oregon residents who have demonstrated financial need and who are disabled or physically handicapped
$ Given: In 1989, 148 grants totaling $70,190 were awarded to individuals; range, $25 - $1,500; general range, $100 - $1,000; average, $410
Application Information: Write for application guidelines; formal application required
Deadline: None
Contact: William K. Shepherd, President

PENNSYLVANIA

Margaret Baker Memorial Fund Trust
Mellon Bank (East) N.A.
P.O. Box 7236
Philadelphia, PA 19101-7236
APPLICATION ADDRESS:
P.O. Box 663
Phoenixville, PA 19460

Description: Financial aid to handicapped children under age 14, and to widows and single women over age 30.
Restrictions: Limited to residents of the Phoenixville, Pennsylvania area
$ Given: Grants range, $108 - $750
Application Information: Send a letter including the applicant's age, income, infirmity (if any), and other supportive material, plus the name of a person who can verify the request
Deadline: Applications accepted throughout the year; awards usually made in July and November
Contact: L. Darlington Lessig, Treasurer

Addison H. Gibson Foundation
Six PPG Place
Suite 860
Pittsburgh, PA 15222
(412) 261-1611

Description: Funds to cover hospital and medical costs for individuals with "correctable physical difficulties."
Restrictions: Limited to residents of western Pennsylvania, with emphasis on Allegheny County
$ Given: Grants range, $60 - $12,000
Application Information: Applicants must be referred by a medical professional; formal application required; medical professional must provide name, age, sex, and address of person for whom funding is sought, describe the nature of recommended medical assistance, and provide the name of the patient's primary physician; grants are made directly to the medical institution providing services; write for further information; formal application required; interview required
Deadline: None
Contact: Charlotte G. Kisseleff, Secretary

James T. Hambay Foundation
Dauphin Deposit Bank &
Trust Company
P.O. Box 2961
Harrisburg, PA 17105
(717) 255-2174

Description: Medical and day care expense aid to financially distressed children under 18 years of age
Restrictions: Residents of Harrisburg, Pennsylvania and vicinity
$ Given: In 1977, 24 grants totaling $25,230 were awarded to individuals; range of $35 - $5,150 per award.
Application Information: Initial approach by letter, including medical expense and income information
Deadline: None
Contact: Joseph A. Macri, Trust Officer, Dauphin Deposit Bank & Trust Company

William B. Lake Foundation
Fidelity Bank, N.A.
Broad and Walnut Streets
3MBO
Philadelphia, PA 19109
(215) 985-7320

Description: Aid to individuals suffering from respiratory diseases
Restrictions: Limited to residents of the Philadelphia, PA
$ Given: In FY90, an unspecified number of grants totaling $30,000 were awarded to individuals
Application Information: Initial contact by letter; please include details of physical conditions and supporting documents
Deadlines: May 1 and November 1
Contact: Maureen B. Evans, Secretary-Treasurer

Quin (Robert D. and Margaret W.) Foundation
Hazleton National Bank
101 West Broad Street
Hazleton, PA 18201

Description: Grants for medication, dental work, clothing, and day care for students under 20 years of age.
Restrictions: Limited to individuals who are at least one-year residents of an area within a ten-mile radius of the Hazleton, Pennsylvania City Hall
$ Given: In 1988, 66 grants totaling $15,367 were awarded; range, $35 - $900
Application Information: Initial approach by letter
Deadline: None
Contact: N/A

Otto Sussman Trust
P.O. Box 1374
Trainsmeadow Station
Flushing, NY 11370-9998

Description: Financial assistance for medical bills and care-giving expenses to individuals with serious or terminal illnesses.
Restrictions: Limited to residents of New York, New Jersey, Oklahoma, and Pennsylvania
$ Given: Grants range, $329 - $4,000
Application Information: Write letter requesting application form and guidelines; explain circumstances of need; formal application required
Deadline: None
Contact: Edward S. Miller, Trustee

PRIVATE FOUNDATION FUNDING

. . . .

RHODE ISLAND

Inez Sprague Trust
c/o Rhode Island Hospital
Trust Bank
One Hospital Trust Plaza
Providence, RI 02903
(401) 278-8700

Description: Financial assistance and medical expenses for needy individuals
Restrictions: Limited to residents of Rhode Island
$ Given: In FY89, 23 grants totaling $6,000 were awarded to individuals; range, $70 - $1,500
Application Information: Initial contact by letter
Deadline: None
Contact: Trustee

SOUTH CAROLINA

Graham Memorial Fund
308 West Main Street
Bennettsville, SC 29512
(803) 479-6804

Description: Grants for medical assistance and general welfare
Restrictions: Limited to residents of Bennettsville, South Carolina
$ Given: In FY89, 37 grants totaling $11,200 were awarded to individuals; range, $200 - $500
Application Information: Formal application required
Deadline: June 1
Contact: Chairman

TENNESSEE

State Industries Foundation
P.O. Box 307
Old Ferry Road
Ashland City, TN 37015
(615) 244-7040

Description: Financial assistance to needy individuals in Tennessee, including State Industries employees
Restrictions: Limited to residents of Tennessee
$ Given: Grants range, $1 - $400; average, $150
Application Information: Write or call for guidelines
Deadline: None
Contact: Joseph P. Lanier, Manager

TEXAS

F.V. Hall, Jr. & Marylou Hall Children's Crisis Foundation
c/o NCNB Texas National Bank
P.O. Box 830241
Dallas, TX 75283-0241

Description: Assistance to infants and children in crisis, or in a situation of critical need or want.
Restrictions: Limited to children under the age of 12 who were either born in Tom Green County, Texas, or who have been physically in residence for more than 12 consecutive months, and whose parents or guardians have no financial resources available to meet the child's needs
$ Given: In FY89, an unspecified number of grants totaling $80,400 were awarded to individuals
Application Information: Formal application required; interviews sometimes required
Deadline: None
Contact: Alice J. Gayle, Trust Officer, NCNB Texas National Bank

Walter Hightower Foundation
c/o Texas Commerce Bank-El Paso
P.O. Drawer 140
El Paso, TX 79980
(915) 546-6515

Description: Funding for medical, dental, and vision treatment, prescriptions, orthopedic devices, and speech therapy to children.
Restrictions: Limited to services provided in west Texas and southern New Mexico
$ Given: In 1988, 657 grants totaling $109,000 were awarded to individuals; range of $10 - $3,600 per award
Application Information: Initial contact by letter; formal application required
Deadline: July 1
Contact: Terry Crenshaw, Charitable Services Officer, Texas Commerce Bank-El Paso

Sunnyside Foundation, Inc.
8609 Northwest Plaza Drive
Suite 201
Dallas, TX 75225
(214) 692-5686

Description: Short-term assistance for underprivileged children
Restrictions: Limited to residents of Texas
$ Given: In 1988, 33 grants for welfare assistance totaling $40,200 were awarded; range, $40 - $4,350
Application Information: Formal application required
Deadline: None
Contact: Mary Rothenflue, Executive Director

PRIVATE FOUNDATION FUNDING

. . . .

VIRGINIA

**Harrison & Conrad
Memorial Trust**
c/o Sovran Bank, N.A.
P.O. Box 26903
Arlington, Ca 22204
APPLICATION ADDRESS:
c/o Loudoun Memorial
Hospital
Office of the Administrator
70 West Cornwall Street
Leesburg, VA 22075
(703) 777-3300

Description: Financial assistance to children afflicted with crippling diseases (e.g., muscular dystrophy and polio).
Restrictions: Residents of Leesburg or Loudoun County, Virginia whose parents cannot afford medical treatment
$ Given: In FY88, 1 grant of $77,700 was awarded.
Application Information: Initial contact by letter; interviews required
Deadline: April 1
Contact: N/A

**A.C. Needles Trust Fund
Hospital Care**
c/o Dominion Trust Company
P.O. Box 13327
Roanoke, VA 24040

Description: Grants for hospital care to financially distressed individuals
Restrictions: Limited to individuals in the Roanoke, Virginia area
$ Given: In 1988, 15 grants totaling $45,620; range, $710 - $9,450
Application Information: Write for guidelines
Deadline: N/A
Contact: N/A

WASHINGTON

G.M.L. Foundation, Inc.
P.O. Box 848
Port Angeles, WA 98362

Description: Grants to individuals who need medical help
Restrictions: Limited to residents of Clallam County, Washington
$ Given: Grants totaling $12,275 awarded to individuals
Application Information: Write for guidelines
Deadline: N/A
Contact: Graham Ralston, Secretary

George T. Welch Testamentary Trust
c/o Baker-Boyer National Bank
P.O. Box 1796
Walla Walla, WA 99362
(509) 525-2000

Description: Medical assistance for financially distressed individuals
Restrictions: Limited to residents of Walla Walla County, WA
$ Given: In FY89, 29 welfare assistance grants totaling $21,980 were awarded to individuals; range, $53 - $1,500
Application Information: Formal application required
Deadlines: February 20, May 20, August 20, and November 20
Contact: Bettie Loiacono, Trust Officer

WEST VIRGINIA

Good Shepherd Foundation, Inc.
Route 4, Box 349
Kinston, NC 28501-9317
(919) 569-3241

Description: Financial assistance for medical expenses
Restrictions: Limited to residents of Trent Township, West Virginia
$ Given: Grants range, $1,130 - $2,500
Application Information: Initial contact by letter; formal application required
Deadline: None
Contact: Sue White, Secretary-Treasurer

Jamey Harless Foundation, Inc.
Drawer D
Gilbert, WV 25621
(304) 664-3227

Description: Loans and grants to financially distressed families
Restrictions: Limited to residents of the Gilbert, West Virginia area
$ Given: Distress grants totaling $4,720 awarded to individuals; distress loans totaling $5,600 made to individuals
Application Information: Initial contact by letter; formal application required
Deadline: None
Contact: Sharon Murphy, Secretary

WISCONSIN

Edward Rutledge Charity
P.O. Box 758
Chippewa Falls, WI 54729
(715) 723-6618

Description: Grants and loans to the needy
Restrictions: Limited to residents of Chippewa County, Wisconsin
$ Given: In FY90, 235 relief assistance grants totaling $16,285 were awarded to individuals; range, $5 - $600
Application Information: Formal application required
Deadline: July 1
Contact: John Frampton, President

PRIVATE FOUNDATION FUNDING

• •

WYOMING

The Gorgen (Peter and Anna) Fund Charitable Trust
141 South Main Street
Buffalo, WY 82834-1824
(307) 684-2211
ADDITIONAL ADDRESS:
c/o William J. Kirven
104 Fort Street
Buffalo, WY 82834
(307) 684-2248

Description: Medical, dental, and optical service grants; payment made directly to service provider.
Restrictions: Limited to children residing in Johnson County, Wyoming
$ Given: In 1988, 32 grants totaling $5,350 were awarded; range, $15 - $500
Application Information: Initial approach by letter, stating financial need
Deadline: None
Contact: Robert R. Holt, Trustee

Perkins (B.F. & Rose H.) Foundation
P.O. Box 1064
Sheridan, WY 82801
(307) 674-8871

Description: Medical assistance grants to children ages 2-20
Restrictions: Limited to individuals who have been residents of Sheridan, Wyoming the last 2 consecutive years
$ Given: In 1989, 165 medical grants totaling $50,097 were awarded; general range, $25 - $1,000
Application Information: Write for application forms for both individual and physician; interviews required
Deadline: Completed forms must be received by the first week of the month prior to treatment
Contact: Margaret Sweem, Manager

PRIVATE FOUNDATION FUNDING—NO GEOGRAPHICAL RESTRICTIONS

Bendheim (Charles and Els) Foundation
One Parker Plaza
Fort Lee, NJ 07024

Description: Grants to individuals for charitable purposes, including aid to the sick and destitute
Restrictions: Applicants must be Jewish and in need of financial assistance
$ Given: In 1989, total giving was $171,880
Application Information: Write for guidelines
Deadline: N/A
Contact: N/A

Broadcasters Foundation, Inc.
320 West 57th Street
New York, NY 10019
(212) 586-2000

Description: Grants to needy members of the broadcast industry and their families
Restrictions: (see above)
$ Given: Grants range from $1,800 - $2,400
Application Information: Formal application required
Deadline: None
Contact: N/A

Eagles Memorial Foundation, Inc.
4710 14th Street West
Bradenton, FL 34207

Description: Financial assistance to children of deceased Eagles servicemen and women, law officers and firefighters for medical, dental, and hospital expenses.
Restrictions: Limited to children (under the age of 18, unmarried and not self supporting) of members of the Fraternal Order of Eagles and the Ladies Auxiliary who have died from injuries or diseases incurred or aggravated while serving (1) in the armed forces, (2) as a law enforcement officer, or (3) as a full-time or volunteer firefighter. Individual recipients receive funds for psychiatric hospital or orthodontic bills, total not to exceed $5,000. No benefits paid for self-inflicted injuries, crime-related injuries, or illnesses/injuries related to drug or alcohol abuse.
$ Given: In FY88, grants for medical and dental expenses totaling $13,420
Application Information: Write for information
Deadline: N/A
Contact: N/A

Island Memorial Medical Fund, Inc.
c/o Richard Purinon
Main Road
Washington Island, WI 54246

Description: Financial assistance to help cover medical expenses for needy individuals; funds paid directly to physicians or treatment facilities.
Restrictions: N/A
$ Given: Grants range, $630 - $8,760
Application Information: Write foundation for application guidelines and current deadline information
Deadline: Varies
Contact: Richard Purinon

PRIVATE FOUNDATION FUNDING

• • • • • • • • • • • • • • • • • •

Henry W. Stoddard Trust
P.O. Box 1365
Arvada, CO 80001
APPLICATION ADDRESS:
7910 Ralston Road, Suite 1
Arvada, CO 80001-1365

Description: Financial assistance for care, health expenses, support, and maintenance of retarded and/or handicapped children. Particular consideration given to parents or other custodians under severe mental, physical, or financial stress because of caregiving to such children. Funding also given to provide for short-term respite care.
Restrictions: No geographic restrictions
$ Given: In FY89, grants to individuals totaled $67,200; grants usually do not exceed $1,000
Application Information: Initial contact by letter
Deadline: N/A
Contact: Wallis L. Campbell, Trustee

Corporate /
Employee
Grants

This chapter contains information about companies and corporations that provide grants or loans for their employees or former employees, including funding to help with the medical expenses of employees' children.

As in the chapter on Private Foundation Funding, the material is organized by state. In some cases, where a corporation has offices in several states, the corporation is listed only under the state in which its headquarters are located. Unless specified in the restrictions, this does *not* mean that monies are available only to employees within that state. Wherever possible, each listing includes a description of what the foundation funds, any restrictions, the total amount of money awarded annually, the number of grants or loans made annually, the range of monies given, the average size of an award, information on how to apply, deadline date(s), and name(s) of contact person(s).

If your company/corporation is not included in this chapter, check with an employee benefits representative or your personnel director to see if your company offers assistance in paying medical expenses for the children of employees.

CORPORATE/EMPLOYEE GRANTS

• •

ARRANGED BY STATE, ACCORDING TO CORPORATE LOCATION

ALABAMA

The Stockham (William H. and Kate F.) Foundation, Inc.
c/o Stockham Valves &
Fittings, Inc.
4000 North Tenth Avenue
P.O. Box 10326
Birmingham, AL 35202

Description: Need-based grants
Restrictions: Strictly limited to **Stockham Valves & Fittings, Inc.** employees, former employees, and their dependents
$ Given: In 1988, 21 grants totaling $18,600 were awarded to individuals; range, $150 - $9,550
Application Information: Initial contact by letter
Deadline: None
Contact: Herbert Stockham, Chairman

CALIFORNIA

A.P. Giannini Foundation for Employees
c/o Bank of America
Personnel Relations
Department No. 3650
P.O. Box 37000
San Francisco, CA 94137
(415) 622-3706

Description: Relief grants to help cover medical bills and other emergency expenses.
Restrictions: Limited to **Bank of America** employees and their families, and to employees of Bank of America subsidiaries
$ Given: In 1989, 3 grants totaling $5,370 were awarded to individuals; range, $790 - $2,640
Application Information: Submit letter of application, including reason for grant request, amount requested, and assessment of applicant's financial status
Deadline: None
Contact: N/A

Clorinda Giannini Memorial Benefit Fund
c/o Bank of America
Trust Department
P.O. Box 37121
San Francisco, CA 94137
(415) 622-3650

Description: Emergency assistance grants for illness, accident disability, surgery, medical and nursing care, hospitalization, financial difficulties, and loss of income.
Restrictions: Limited to **Bank of America** employees
$ Given: In FY89, 25 grants totaling $27,900 were awarded to individuals; range, $35 - $6,200; general range, $800 - $2,000
Application Information: Initial contact by letter
Deadline: None
Contact: Susan Morales

Pfaffinger Foundation
Times Mirror Square
Los Angeles, CA 90053
(213) 237-5743

Description: Need-based grants
Restrictions: Limited to employees and former employees of **The Times Mirror Company**
$ Given: In 1987, 354 grants totaling $1.74 million were awarded to individuals; range, $13 - $40,550
Application Information: Initial contact by letter; formal application required; final notification usually in one week after application is received
Deadline: None
Contact: James C. Kelly, President

Plitt Southern Theatres, Inc. Employees Fund
1801 Century Park East
Suite 1225
Los Angeles, CA 90067

Description: Welfare assistance grants
Restrictions: Limited to employees of **Plitt Southern Theatres**
$ Given: In 1988, 77 grants totaling $226,900 were awarded to individuals; range, $200 - $10,000
Application Information: Write for guidelines
Deadline: N/A
Contact: Joe S. Jackson, President

CONNECTICUT

AMAX Aid Fund, Inc.
AMAX Center
Greenwich, CT 06836

Description: Financial assistance to needy employees, former employees, and families of deceased employees of **AMAX, Inc.** and its subsidiaries.
Restrictions: Individuals earning an annual salary from AMAX or receiving an AMAX pension are not eligible
$ Given: In 1987, 4 grants totaling $7,150 were awarded to individuals; no grants were awarded in 1988
Application Information: Write for guidelines
Deadline: N/A
Contact: David George Ball, Senior Vice President

IDAHO

Morrison-Knudsen Employees Foundation, Inc.
One Morrison-Knudsen Plaza
Boise, ID 83729
(208) 386-5000

Description: Need-based assistance
Restrictions: Limited to employees of **Morrison-Knudsen**
$ Given: In 1989, 24 grants totaling $114,200 were awarded to individuals; range, $700 - $8,900
Application Information: Write or call for guidelines
Deadline: None
Contact: M.M. Puckett, Foundation Manager

CORPORATE/EMPLOYEE GRANTS

• • • • • • • • • • • • • • • • • • • •

ILLINOIS

**The Clara Abbott
Foundation**
One Abbott Park Road
Abbott Park, IL 60064-3500
(312) 937-1091

Description: Relief grants and loans to employees and retired employees of Abbott Laboratories, as well as to members of their families.
Restrictions: Limited to employees, retirees and families of employees of **Abbott Laboratories**
$ Given: In 1988, 516 relief grants totaling $868,000 were awarded to individuals
Application Information: Write or call for guidelines
Deadline: None
Contact: David C. Jefferies, Executive Director

Walgreen Benefit Fund
200 Wilmot Road
Deerfield, IL 60015
(708) 940-2931

Description: Welfare assistance grants
Restrictions: Limited to **Walgreen** employees and their families
$ Given: In FY90, an unspecified number of grants totaling $305,000 were awarded to individuals
Application Information: Initial contact by letter
Deadline: None
Contact: Edward H. King, Vice President

MASSACHUSETTS

**Henry Hornblower Fund,
Inc.**
Box 2365
Boston, MA 02169
(617) 589-3286

Description: Need-based grants
Restrictions: Limited to current and former employees of **Hornblower & Weeks**
$ Given: In 1988, two grants totaling $6,000 were awarded to individuals; range, $1,000 - $5,000
Application Information: Initial contact by letter
Deadline: None
Contact: Nathan N. Withington, President

MICHIGAN

Hudson-Webber Foundation
333 West Fort Street
Suite 1310
Detroit, MI 48226
(313) 963-7777

Description: Counseling services and last-resort financial assistance. Grants provided primarily in cases involving problems with physical or emotional health, and in financial emergencies.
Restrictions: Limited to employees and qualified retired employees of the **J.L. Hudson Company**
$ Given: In 1989, 92 grants totaling $78,850 were awarded to individuals; general range, $500 - $1,000
Application Information: Formal application required for review by the foundation's trustees; interviews required
Deadline: None
Contact: Gilbert Hudson, President

MISSOURI

**Butler Manufacturing
Company Foundation**
Penn Valley Park
P.O. Box 419917
BMA Tower
Kansas City, MO 64141-0197
(816) 968-3208

Description: Hardship grants to aid individuals in emergency financial distress due to serious illness or catastrophic property damage.
Restrictions: Limited to **Butler Manufacturing Company** employees, retirees and their dependents
$ Given: In 1989, 3 hardship grants totaling $10,650 were awarded; range, $650 - $8,000; general range, $500 - $2,000
Application Information: Write for application guidelines and program information; interviews required
Deadline: None
Contact: Barbara Lee Fay, Foundation Administrator

Hall Family Foundations
c/o Charitable and Crown
Investment
Department 323
P.O. Box 419580
Kansas City, MO 64141-6580
(816) 274-8516

Description: Grants for emergency relief assistance
Restrictions: Strictly limited to employees of **Hallmark**
$ Given: In 1988, total giving was $1.7 million; relief assistance subtotal unspecified
Application Information: Write or call for guidelines
Deadline: N/A
Contact: Margaret H. Pence, Director/Program Officer

CORPORATE/EMPLOYEE GRANTS

Kansas City Life Employees Welfare Fund
3520 Broadway
Kansas City, MO 64111-2565
(816) 753-7000

Description: Medical assistance grants
Restrictions: Limited to **Kansas City Life** employees and their spouses and/or dependents
$ Given: In 1988, 2 grants totaling $4,263 were awarded to individuals; range, $950 - $3,313
Application Information: Initial contact by letter
Deadline: None
Contact: Dennis M. Gaffney

David May Employees Trust Fund
Sixth and Olive Streets
St. Louis, MO 63101

Description: Need-based grants
Restrictions: Limited to employees and former employees of the **May Department Stores Company**
$ Given: In 1988, an unspecified number of grants totaling $11,500 were awarded to individuals
Application Information: Write for guidelines
Deadline: N/A
Contact: N/A

Edward F. Swinney Foundation
c/o Boatmen's First National Bank of Kansas City
P.O. Box 419038
Kansas City, MO 64183
(816) 234-7481

Description: Need-based grants
Restrictions: Limited to employees of **Boatmen's First National Bank of Kansas City**
$ Given: In 1988, 138 grants totaling $52,800 were awarded to individuals; range, $9 - $5,600
Application Information: Formal application required
Deadline: None
Contact: David P. Ross, Trust Officer

NEW YORK

Richard D. Brown Trust B
c/o Chemical Bank
Administrative Services Department
30 Rockefeller Plaza
New York, NY 10112
(212) 621-2143

Description: Need-based loans
Restrictions: Limited to employees of **Chemical Bank**
$ Given: In 1988, an unspecified number of loans to individuals totaling $10,700 were made
Application Information: Recipients chosen by staff benefits committee
Deadline: None
Contact: Mrs. B. Strohmeier

The Ernst & Young Foundation
277 Park Avenue
New York, NY 10172

Description: Financial assistance grants to employees and their families
Restrictions: Limited to **Ernst & Young** employees and their families
$ Given: In 1988, one relief grant for $2,400 was awarded
Application Information: Write for guidelines
Deadline: N/A
Contact: Bruce J. Mantia, Administrator

McCrory Corporation Needy & Worthy Employees Trust
c/o Chase Manhattan Bank, N.A.
Tax Services Division
1211 Avenue of the Americas
36th Floor
New York, NY 10036

Description: Need-based grants
Restrictions: Limited to worthy employees of the **McCrory Corporation**
$ Given: In 1988, 2 grants totaling $12,444 were awarded to individuals; range, $5,000 - $7,444
Application Information: Write for guidelines
Deadline: N/A
Contact: Larry Tynan

United Merchants & Manufacturers Employees Welfare Foundation
1407 Broadway
6th Floor
New York, NY 10018-5103

Description: Need-based grants
Restrictions: Limited to current and former employees of **United Merchants & Manufacturers, Inc.**, and to members of their families
$ Given: In FY89, 14 grants totaling $9,800 were awarded to individuals; range, $375 - $825
Application Information: Write for guidelines
Deadline: None
Contact: Lawrence Marx, Jr., Trustee

NORTH CAROLINA

Burlington Industries Foundation
P.O. Box 21207
3330 West Friendly Avenue
Greensboro, NC 27420
(919) 379-2515

Description: Disaster aid
Restrictions: Limited to **Burlington Industries** employees and their families; primary focus of giving in North Carolina, South Carolina and Virginia
$ Given: In FY89, 54 grants totaling $29,250 were awarded to individuals; range, $250 - $1,000
Application Information: Call or write for program information; interviews upon request
Deadline: None
Contact: Park R. Davidson, Executive Director

CORPORATE/EMPLOYEE GRANTS

• • • • • • • • • • • • • • • • • • • •

OHIO

National Machinery Foundation, Inc.
Greenfield Street
P.O. Box 747
Tiffin, OH 44883
(419) 447-5211

Description: Need-based grants
Restrictions: Limited to former employees of **National Machinery** and to other financially distressed individuals in Seneca County, Ohio
$ Given: In 1988, 205 relief grants totaling $69,950 were awarded to individuals; range, $150 - $4,000
Application Information: Initial contact by letter
Deadline: N/A
Contact: D.B. Bero, Administrator

Richman Brothers Foundation
Box 657
Chagrin Falls, OH 44022
(216) 247-5426

Description: Relief assistance grants
Restrictions: Limited to employees, pensioners, widows, and children of employees of the **Richman Brothers Company**; preference to individuals in Cleveland, Ohio
$ Given: In 1989, 192 grants totaling $45,500 were awarded to individuals; range, $100 - $2,000
Application Information: Write for guidelines; formal application required
Deadline: November 15
Contact: Richard R. Moore, President

OREGON

Journal Publishing Company Employees Welfare Fund, Inc.
P.O. Box 3168
Portland, OR 97208

Description: Welfare assistance grants
Restrictions: Limited to employees of **Journal Publishing Company**
$ Given: In FY89, 20 grants totaling $55,950 were awarded to individuals; range, $1,200 - $3,600
Application Information: Write for guidelines
Deadline: None
Contact: N/A

PENNSYLVANIA

Vang Memorial Foundation
P.O. Box 11727
Pittsburgh, PA 15228
(412) 563-0261

Description: Grants-in-aid
Restrictions: Limited to past, present and future employees of **George Vang, Inc.** and related companies, and their dependents
$ Given: In 1988, 15 grants totaling $29,233 were awarded to individuals; range, $670 - $5,251; general range, $720 - $2,000
Application Information: Submit introductory letter, including name, address and telephone number of applicant and specifying type of grant requested and basis of need
Deadline: None
Contact: E.J. Hosko, Treasurer

SOUTH CAROLINA

**Burlington Industries
Foundation**
P.O. Box 21207
3330 West Friendly Avenue
Greensboro, NC 27420
(919) 379-2515

Description: Disaster aid
Restrictions: Limited to **Burlington Industries** employees and their families; primary focus of giving in North Carolina, South Carolina and Virginia
$ Given: In FY89, 54 grants totaling $29,250 were awarded to individuals; range, $250 - $1,000
Application Information: Call or write for program information; interviews upon request
Deadline: None
Contact: Park R. Davidson, Executive Director

TEXAS

**Amon G. Carter Star
Telegram Employees Fund**
P.O. Box 17480
Fort Worth, TX 76102
(817) 332-3535

Description: Medical assistance grants and pension supplements
Restrictions: Limited to employees of the **Fort Worth Star-Telegram**, **KXAS-TV**, and **WBAP-Radio**
$ Given: In FY89, 28 welfare assistance grants totaling $233,000 were awarded; range, $840 - $7,960
Application Information: Initial contact by letter
Deadline: None
Contact: Nenetta Tatum, President

65

CORPORATE/EMPLOYEE GRANTS

. . . .

The Mary L. Peyton Foundation
Bassett Tower
Suite 908
303 Texas Avenue
El Paso, TX 79901
(915) 533-9698

Description: Assistance grants for medical care, as well as for food, clothing, and other necessities. Funding given to individuals who cannot earn their livelihood due to physical or mental disabilities, due to being under-age, or due to old age.
Restrictions: Strictly limited to citizens of El Paso, Texas, with preference to children of current and former employees of **Peyton Packing Company**
$ Given: In FY89, 790 grants totaling $173,550 were awarded to individuals; range, $8 - $1,600 per award
Application Information: Write a letter explaining the circumstances causing financial need and including an itemization of services/items required
Deadline: None
Contact: James Day, Executive Director

VIRGINIA

Burlington Industries Foundation
P.O. Box 21207
3330 West Friendly Avenue
Greensboro, NC 27420
(919) 379-2515

Description: Disaster aid
Restrictions: Limited to **Burlington Industries** employees and their families; primary focus of giving in North Carolina, South Carolina and Virginia
$ Given: In FY89, 54 grants totaling $29,250 were awarded to individuals; range, $250 - $1,000
Application Information: Call or write for program information; interviews upon request
Deadline: None
Contact: Park R. Davidson, Executive Director

COMPANIES WITH EMPLOYEES NATIONWIDE AND ABROAD

The Correspondents Fund
c/o Rosenman & Cohen
575 Madison Avenue
New York, NY 10022-2511
APPLICATION ADDRESS: c/o The New York Times, 229 West 43rd Street, New York, NY 10036

Description: Emergency grants
Restrictions: Limited to individuals who have worked in the U.S. press, television, radio, news, film, and other U.S. news organizations within or outside the U.S., and to individuals who have worked in the foreign press or other foreign news organizations, and to their dependents
$ Given: In FY89, 3 grants totaling $8,200 were awarded to individuals; range, $2,500 - $3,000
Application Information: Submit an introductory letter, including details of the circumstances for which aid is requested
Deadline: None
Contact: James L. Greenfield, President

Roger L. Von Amelunxen Foundation, Inc.
83-21 Edgerton Blvd.
Jamaica, NY 11432
(718) 641-4800

Description: Welfare assistance grants
Restrictions: Limited to financially distressed families of **U.S. Customs Service** employees
$ Given: In FY89, 9 welfare assistance grants totaling $21,000 were awarded to individuals; range, $500 - $5,000
Application Information: Submit letter with proof of relationship to U.S. Customs Service employee
Deadline: August 1
Contact: Karen Donnelly, Vice President

Flow-through
Funding

Flow-through funding is different from any other kind of grant funding described in this book. **Flow-through funding is indirect funding**; that is, the foundations listed in this chapter do not provide money directly to individuals, but instead give money to nonprofit organizations, which, in turn, pass funds along to people in need. The nonprofit organizations — which may be hospitals, hospices, or other types of support agencies — serve as sponsors for the individuals who require financial assistance.

Individuals cannot apply directly to these foundations for funding. The foundations listed in this chapter accept applications only from nonprofit organizations. In order to receive funds from any of the foundations listed here, you must work through a sponsoring nonprofit organization.

Why should you bother with a sponsor? The number of foundations included in this chapter should give you an idea of the vast amounts of grant money made available as flow-through funding. Grant money awarded to your nonprofit sponsor may be used as reimbursement for your direct medical expenses, such as hospital bills, doctors' fees, prescription drugs, home care, institutional care, and rehabilitative care. Many times, monies awarded to a hospital or large organization are applied to the needs of more than one person; one grant award usually benefits a group of individuals. In asking your nonprofit sponsor to contact these foundations on your behalf, you are, in a sense, promoting the interests of other individuals served by the sponsor. However, don't let this discourage you from making use of the information in this chapter.

FLOW-THROUGH FUNDING

• •

How do you go about finding a nonprofit sponsor?
Check any local directory of nonprofit organizations
(your local library will usually have such directories in
its collection, perhaps in a community services section).
Contact local city-wide consortium-styled associations
operating in your area of interest, such as the United
Way, health planning bodies, federations, and so on.
Speak to their directors or public information officers
and elicit their suggestions for possible sponsors. Also
check national organizational reference books, such as
the *Encyclopedia of Associations*, for other potential candi-
dates. Another approach to finding a nonprofit sponsor
is to work with one of the associations that addresses
the needs of children with specific diseases or disorders.
Check the "Associations" chapter of this book for the
names, addresses and telephone numbers of such associations.

How to Apply: Although you cannot apply directly to
any of the foundations contained in this chapter, your
background work here can be extremely helpful to your
sponsor organization. Use the information provided in
this chapter to identify foundations that seem to address your specific situation. Following your non-profit
sponsor's directions, write to the appropriate foundations to request information, including application guidelines. If the hospital or health care facility itself will
serve as your sponsor, you should meet with the case
manager or social worker responsible for investigating
the financial matters associated with your child's care.
Share any information you have received from potential
funding sources. The case manager or social worker can
determine whether or not the foundations offer flow-
through funding to meet your needs. If another type of
organization is acting as your sponsor, follow the proto-
col established by that organization.

ALABAMA

Child Health Foundation
P.O. Box 530964
Birmingham, AL 35253
(205) 251-9966

Description: The foundation's objective is to reduce illness and disease in children.
Restrictions: Giving primarily in Alabama
$ Given: In 1988, $66,654 in group grants; range, $5,000 - $31,200; and $50,250 in grants to individuals
Application Information: Write for application guidelines; see the important information in the chapter introduction about the need for institutional affiliation.
Deadline: August 31
Contact: Dr. Sergio Stagno, Executive Director

Hargis (Estes H. & Florence Parker) Charitable Foundation
317 20th St. North
P.O. Box 370404
Birmingham, AL 35237
(205) 251-2881

Description: Funding for health and youth services
Restrictions: Limited primarily to Tennessee and Alabama
$ Given: In FY88, seven grants totaling $395,374; range, $300 - $376,075
Application Information: Write for application guidelines; see the important information in the chapter introduction about the need for institutional affiliation.
Deadline: May 1
Contact: Gerald D. Colvin, Jr., Chair

Hasbro Children's Foundation
32 West 23rd St.
New York, NY 10010
(212) 645-2400

Description: Funding designated for improving children's quality of life; emphasis on health care programs, including pediatric AIDS programs, and on education for the handicapped.
Restrictions: Funding to direct service providers is given on a nationwide basis; limited to programs involving children under the age of 12
$ Given: In 1988, 54 grants totaling $1.7 million were awarded; range of $500 - $150,000 per award; average range of $5,000 - $150,000 per award
Application Information: Write for application guidelines; see the important information in the chapter introduction about the need for institutional affiliation.
Deadlines: Two months prior to board meetings (board meets in February, June, and October)
Contact: Eve Weiss, Executive Director

FLOW-THROUGH FUNDING

• • • • • • • • • • • • • • • • • • • •

D.W. McMillan
Foundation
329 Belleville Ave.
Brewton, AL 36426
(205) 867-4881
APPLICATION ADDRESS:
P.O. Box 867
Brewton, AL 36427

Description: Funds local health and welfare organizations; funds only those programs giving direct aid.
Restrictions: Limited to Escambia County, Alabama, and Escambia County, Florida
$ Given: In 1988, 21 grants totaling $392,000; range, $1,500 - $60,000
Application Information: Write for application guidelines; see the important information in the chapter introduction about the need for institutional affiliation.
Deadline: December 1
Contact: Ed Leigh McMillan, II, Managing Trustee

Monsanto Fund
800 No. Lindbergh Blvd.
St. Louis, MO 63167
(314) 694-4596

Description: Although the $8 million corporate giving program focuses on education, the fund also provides significant support to hospitals and health service agencies.
Restrictions: Major funding emphasis on St. Louis, Missouri, with additional giving in the following areas of corporate operations: Alabama, California, Florida, Georgia, Idaho, Illinois, Massachusetts, Michigan, Missouri, New Jersey, North Carolina, Ohio, South Carolina, Texas, and West Virginia. No monies for religious organizations.
$ Given: In 1988, corporate giving totaled $8.3 million; average range of $100 - $5,000 per award
Application Information: Write for application guidelines; see the important information in the chapter introduction about the need for institutional affiliation.
Deadline: None
Contact: John L. Mason, President

ALASKA

ARCO Foundation
515 South Flower St.
Los Angeles, CA 90071
(213) 486-3342

Description: Funds various health and youth organizations, including a satellite dental clinic program.
Restrictions: Giving limited to areas of operations, including Los Angeles, California; Anchorage, Alaska; and Dallas, Texas
$ Given: In 1988, 1,539 grants totaling $12,213,500; average range, $2,500 - $25,000
Application Information: Write for application guidelines; see the important information in the chapter introduction about the need for institutional affiliation.
Deadline: None
Contact: Eugene R. Wilson, President

Hasbro Children's Foundation

Description: (see full listing information under Alabama)

Meyer Memorial Trust
1515 S.W. Fifth Ave.
Suite 500
Portland, OR 97201
(503) 228-5512

Description: As one example of its various types of funding and specifically-targeted programming, the trust provides grants through the Children at Risk program.
Restrictions: The Children at Risk program funds projects in Oregon, Washington, Idaho, Montana, and Alaska; no monies for religious use
$ Given: In FY90, 209 grants totaling $11.9 million were awarded; range of $500 - $2 million per award; average range of $20,000 - $200,000 per award; these figures account for funding through all programs
Application Information: Write for application guidelines; see the important information in the chapter introduction about the need for institutional affiliation.
Deadlines: April 1 and October 1 for the Children at Risk program
Contact: Charles S. Rooks, Executive Director

ARIZONA

Arizona Community Foundation
4350 East Camelback Rd.
Suite 216 C
Phoenix, AZ 85018
(602) 952-9954

Description: Funds children's mental health, youth agencies, health agencies, organizations for the handicapped, and other human services programs.
Restrictions: Giving limited to Arizona
$ Given: In 1989, 182 grants totaling $2,017,865; average range, $1,000 - $10,000
Application Information: Write for application guidelines; see the important information in the chapter introduction about the need for institutional affiliation.
Deadlines: February 1, June 1, October 1
Contact: Stephen D. Mittenthal, President

FLOW-THROUGH FUNDING

• •

FHP Foundation
401 East Ocean Blvd.
Suite 206
Long Beach, CA 90802-
4933
(310) 590-8655

Description: Funding for health care services, including programs for the chronically ill and primary health care projects in underserved areas.
Restrictions: Funding focused in southern California, Utah, New Mexico, and Arizona
$ Given: In FY89, 17 grants totaling $773,064 were awarded; range of $2,900 - $89,000 per award
Application Information: Write for application guidelines; see the important information in the chapter introduction about the need for institutional affiliation.
Deadlines: February 15, May 15, August 15, and November 15
Contact: Sandra Lund Gavin, Executive Director

The Flinn Foundation
3300 North Central Ave.
Suite 2300
Phoenix, AZ 85012
(602) 274-9000

Description: Funding interests include enhancing health care availability to young children and to parenting and pregnant teens.
Restrictions: Limited to residents of Arizona
$ Given: In 1989, 97 grants totaling $4,595,750; average range, $20,000 - $100,000
Application Information: Write for application guidelines; see the important information in the chapter introduction about the need for institutional affiliation.
Deadline: None
Contact: John W. Murphy, Executive Director

Hasbro Children's Foundation

Description: (see full listing information under Alabama)

US WEST Foundation
7800 East Orchard Rd.
Suite 300
Englewood, CO 80111
(303) 793-6661

Description: Funding emphasis on health and human services, including children's clinics in Seattle, Washington and Salt Lake City, Utah.
Restrictions: Limited to Arizona, Colorado, Iowa, Idaho, Minnesota, Montana, North Dakota, Nebraska, New Mexico, South Dakota, Oregon, Utah, Washington, and Wyoming
$ Given: In 1989, 3,622 grants totaling $18,266,190; average range, $500 - $10,000
Application Information: Write for application guidelines; see the important information in the chapter introduction about the need for institutional affiliation.
Deadline: None
Contact: L.J. Nash, Director of Administration

ARKANSAS

The Chatlos Foundation, Inc.
P.O. Box 915048
Longwood, FL 32791-5048
(407) 862-5077

Description: Funding interests include hospitals, health agencies, and child welfare, including children's hospitals in Arkansas and Minnesota.
Restrictions: Only one grant to any organization within a twelve-month period
$ Given: In 1988, 174 grants totaling $2,488,325; average range, $5,000 - $25,000
Application Information: Write for application guidelines; see the important information in the chapter introduction about the need for institutional affiliation.
Deadline: None
Contact: William J. Chatlos, President

Hasbro Children's Foundation

Description: (see full listing information under Alabama)

Levi Strauss Foundation
1155 Battery St.
P.O. Box 7215
San Francisco, CA 94111
(415) 544-1378

Description: Focus is to improve human services through direct grants, including a grant to Children's Hospital in Oakland, CA.
Restrictions: Limited to Arkansas, California, Georgia, Kentucky, Mississippi, Tennessee, Nevada, New Mexico, North Carolina, Texas, and Virginia
$ Given: In 1988, 258 grants totaling $2,936,000; range, $100 - $79,600
Application Information: Write for application guidelines; see the important information in the chapter introduction about the need for institutional affiliation.
Deadline: None
Contact: Martha Montag Brown, Director of Contributions

CALIFORNIA

The Ahmanson Foundation
9215 Wilshire Blvd.
Beverly Hills, CA 90210
(310) 278-0770

Description: Grant recipients include hospitals and youth service organizations
Restrictions: Emphasis on the Los Angeles area of southern CA.
$ Given: In FY89, 406 grants totaling $20,150,353; range, $300 - $1,850,000; average range, $10,000 - $25,000
Application Information: Write for application guidelines; see the important information in the chapter introduction about the need for institutional affiliation.
Deadline: None
Contact: Lee E. Walcott, Vice President and Managing Director

FLOW-THROUGH FUNDING

• • • • • • • • • • • • • • • • • • • •

ARCO Foundation

Description: (see full listing information under Alaska)

The Bothin Foundation
873 Sutter St.
Suite B
San Francisco, CA
94109
(415) 771-4300

Description: Funding interests include youth, health, and social services.
Restrictions: Emphasis on San Francisco, San Mateo, Marin, and Sonoma Counties in northern California
$ Given: In 1988, 84 grants totaling $664,380; range, $25 - $50,000 per award
Application Information: Write for application guidelines; see the important information in the chapter introduction about the need for institutional affiliation.
Deadlines: 8 weeks prior to board meetings; board meets in February, June and October
Contact: Lyman H. Casey, Executive Director

California Community Foundation
606 South Olive St.
Suite 2400
Los Angeles, CA 90014
(213) 413-4042
ORANGE COUNTY
OFFICE:
13252 Garden Grove Blvd.
Suite 195
Garden Grove, CA 92643
(714) 750-7794

Description: Funding interests include health and medicine, with emphasis on youth and children.
Restrictions: Limited to Los Angeles, Ventura, Riverside, Orange, and San Bernadino counties, California
$ Given: In FY1989, grants totaling $8.69 million; average range, $5,000 - $25,000
Application Information: Write for application guidelines; see the important information in the chapter introduction about the need for institutional affiliation.
Deadline: None
Contact: Jack Shakely, President

The Coca-Cola Foundation, Inc.
One Coca-Cola Plaza, N.W.
Atlanta, GA 30313
(404) 676-2568

Description: Funding interests include health and wellness, including a program for children with arthritis in Atlanta, Georgia.
Restrictions: Limited to Atlanta, Georgia, Los Angeles, California; New York, New York; and Houston, Texas
$ Given: In 1988, 219 grants totaling $5,138,530; average range, $2,500 - $50,000
Application Information: Write for application guidelines; see the important information in the chapter introduction about the need for institutional affiliation.
Deadline: None
Contact: Donald R. Greene, President

• • • • • • • • • • • • • • • • • • • •

S.H. Cowell Foundation
260 California St.
Suite 501
San Francisco, CA
94111
(415) 397-0285

Description: Focus on health programs for adolescents and handicapped children
Restrictions: Limited to northern California
$ Given: In 1989, 152 grants totaling $10,407,130; range, $3,000 - $5,480,570; average range, $20,000 - $100,000
Application Information: Write for application guidelines; see the important information in the chapter introduction about the need for institutional affiliation.
Deadline: None
Contact: Stephanie Wolf, Executive Director

Freeman E. Fairfield Foundation
3610 Long Beach Blvd.
P.O. Box 7798
Long Beach, CA 90807
(310) 427-7219

Description: Supports youth agencies, medical centers and clinics, handicapped and general social services, including child welfare and development.
Restrictions: Limited to Long Beach and Signal Hill, California
$ Given: In 1988, 20 grants totaling $378,486; average range, $5,000 - $20,000
Application Information: Write for application guidelines; see the important information in the chapter introduction about the need for institutional affiliation.
Deadline: May 1
Contact: Edna E. Sellers, Trustee

Fannie Mae Foundation
3900 Wisconsin Ave. N.W.
Washington, DC 20016
(202) 752-6500

Description: Funding interests include housing and community development, and health and social concerns.
Restrictions: Limited to Washington, DC; Pasadena, California; Atlanta, Georgia; Chicago, Illinois; Philadelphia, Pennsylvania; and Dallas, Texas
$ Given: In 1989, 300 grants totaling $1,151,567; range, $100 - $50,000
Application Information: Write for application guidelines; see the important information in the chapter introduction about the need for institutional affiliation.
Deadline: None
Contact: Harriet M. Ivey, Executive Director

FLOW-THROUGH FUNDING

• •

The Favrot Fund
909 Wirt Rd.
No. 101
Houston, TX 77024-3444
(713) 956-4009

Description: Focus on community-based programs for health, the needy, and youth agencies.
Restrictions: Limited to Texas, California, New York, and Washington, DC
$ Given: In 1987, 24 grants totaling $310,000; range, $2,000 - $25,000
Application Information: Write for application guidelines; see the important information in the chapter introduction about the need for institutional affiliation.
Deadline: None
Contact: Mrs. Carol Parker

FHP Foundation

Description: (see full listing information under Arizona)

First Nationwide Bank Corporate Giving Program
700 Market St.
San Francisco, CA 94102
(415) 772-1575

Description: Funds community, social, and health services
Restrictions: Limited to California
$ Given: 220 grants totaling $305,000; range, $150 - $20,000
Application Information: Write for application guidelines; see the important information in the chapter introduction about the need for institutional affiliation.
Deadline: None
Contact: Stephen L. Johnson, Senior Vice President

The Garland (John Jewett & H. Chandler) Foundation
P.O. Box 550
Pasadena, CA 91102-0550

Description: Funds youth agencies, hospitals and health services
Restrictions: Limited to California, with emphasis on Los Angeles
$ Given: In 1986, 50 grants totaling $1,261,500; average range, $5,000 - $20,000
Application Information: Write for application guidelines; see the important information in the chapter introduction about the need for institutional affiliation.
Deadline: None
Contact: N/A

**The William G.
Gilmore Foundation**
120 Montgomery St.
Suite 1880
San Francisco, CA
94104
(415) 546-1400

Description: General purpose funding and emergency funding for health services and AIDS programs, as well as for several other community-based organizations.
Restrictions: Funding focused primarily in California, Oregon and Washington
$ Given: In 1988, 132 grants totaling $766,345 were awarded; range of $200 - $50,000 per award; average range of $500 - $5,000 per award
Application Information: Write for application guidelines; see the important information in the chapter introduction about the need for institutional affiliation.
Deadlines: May 1, November 1
Contact: Faye Wilson, Secretary

**Great American
Corporate Giving
Program**
600 B St.
Suite 800
San Diego, CA 92101
(619) 231-6242

Description: Funds community health care
Restrictions: Limited to California
$ Given: N/A
Application Information: Write for application guidelines; see the important information in the chapter introduction about the need for institutional affiliation.
Deadline: None
Contact: Karen Miller, Community Relations Officer

**Hasbro Children's
Foundation**

Description: (see full listing information under Alabama)

Hedco Foundation
c/o Fitzgerald, Abbott &
Beardsley
1221 BRd.way
21st Floor
Oakland, CA 94612-1837

Description: Funds educational and health service institutions
Restrictions: Limited primarily to California
$ Given: In FY88, 23 grants totaling $1,019,454; range, $500 - $469,160
Application Information: Write for application guidelines; see the important information in the chapter introduction about the need for institutional affiliation.
Deadline: None
Contact: Mary A. Goriup, Foundation Manager

FLOW-THROUGH FUNDING

• • • • • • • • • • • • • • • • • • • •

Jerome Foundation
4020 Bandini Blvd.
Los Angeles, CA 90023
(714) 995-1696
APPLICATION ADDRESS:
2660 West Woodland Dr.
Suite 160
Anaheim, Ca 92801

Description: Funds medical research, services for handicapped children and the blind, and hospitals and health services.
Restrictions: Limited primarily to southern California
$ Given: In 1988, 17 grants totaling $147,383; range, $100 - $124,530
Application Information: Write for application guidelines; see the important information in the chapter introduction about the need for institutional affiliation.
Deadline: None
Contact: Pat Perry

The Fletcher Jones Foundation
One Wilshire Building
Suite 1210
624 South Grand Ave.
Los Angeles, CA 90017
(213) 689-9292

Description: Grants for social services, hospitals, and children's health clinics
Restrictions: Giving limited to California
$ Given: In 1989, 47 grants totaling $4,051,076; average range, $5,000 - $100,000
Application Information: Write for application guidelines; see the important information in the chapter introduction about the need for institutional affiliation.
Deadlines: February, April, August, and October
Contact: John W. Smythe, Executive Director

Levi Strauss Foundation

Description: (see full listing information under Arkansas)

Livingston Memorial Foundation
625 North A St.
Oxnard, CA 93030
(805) 983-0561
MAILING ADDRESS:
P.O. Box 1232
Oxnard, CA 93032

Description: Funding support for health and health-related activites
Restrictions: Limited to Ventura County, California
$ Given: In FY89, 27 grants totaling $313,750; range, $850 - $165,000
Application Information: Write for application guidelines; see the important information in the chapter introduction about the need for institutional affiliation.
Deadline: February 1
Contact: Laura K. McAvoy

• • • • • • • • • • • • • • • • • • • •

Bert William Martin Foundation
c/o The Northern Trust Company
50 South LaSalle St.
Chicago, IL 60675
(312) 630-6000

Description: Funds hospitals and health services
Restrictions: Limited to California and Mount Vernon, Ohio
$ Given: In 1988, 23 grants totaling $147,700; range, $300 - $75,000
Application Information: Write for application guidelines; see the important information in the chapter introduction about the need for institutional affiliation.
Deadline: N/A
Contact: Winifred M. Warden, President

Monsanto Fund

Description: (see full listing information under Alabama)

The San Francisco Foundation
685 Market St.
Suite 910
San Francisco, CA
94105-9716
(415) 543-0223

Description: Funding interests include community health, including a grant to Children's Hospital in Oakland, California.
Restrictions: Limited to San Francisco, San Mateo, Marin, Contra Costa, and Alameda counties, California
$ Given: In FY89, grants totaling $11,124,714; average grant, $20,000
Application Information: Write for application guidelines; see the important information in the chapter introduction about the need for institutional affiliation.
Deadline: None
Contact: Robert M. Fisher, Director

Santa Barbara Foundation
15 East Carillo St.
Santa Barbara, CA
93101
(805) 963-1873

Description: Funding includes social services, youth and health services
Restrictions: Limited to Santa Barbara County, California
$ Given: In 1989, 137 grants totaling $1,692,087
Application Information: Write for application guidelines; see the important information in the chapter introduction about the need for institutional affiliation.
Deadline: None
Contact: Edward R. Spaulding, Executive Director

FLOW-THROUGH FUNDING

• •

The Steele (Harry and Grace) Foundation
441 Old Newport Blvd.
Suite 301
Newport Beach, CA
92663
(714) 631-9158

Description: Funding interests include hospitals and youth clinics
Restrictions: Limited to Orange County, California
$ Given: In FY89, 63 grants totaling $8.3 million; average range, $5,000 - $250,000
Application Information: Write for application guidelines; see the important information in the chapter introduction about the need for institutional affiliation.
Deadline: None
Contact: Marie F. Kowert, Assistant Secretary

Van Nuys (J.B. and Emily) Charities
1800 Ave. of the Stars
Suite 435
Los Angeles, CA 90067
(213) 552-0175

Description: Funds hospitals and health service agencies, as well as child welfare and youth agencies.
Restrictions: Limited primarily to southern California.
$ Given: In 1988, 130 grants totaling $557,355; average, $5,000
Application Information: Write for application guidelines; see the important information in the chapter introduction about the need for institutional affiliation.
Deadline: None
Contact: Robert Gibson Johnson, President

Wood-Claeyssens Foundation
P.O. Box 30547
Santa Barbara, CA
93130-0547
(805) 682-4775

Description: Funds hospitals, health services, social services, and youth agencies.
Restrictions: Limited to California
$ Given: In FY89, 52 grants totaling $298,000; range, $500 - $50,000; average range, $500 - $2,000
Application Information: Write for application guidelines; see the important information in the chapter introduction about the need for institutional affiliation.
Deadline: August 31
Contact: Pierre P. Claeyssens, First Vice President

COLORADO

The Allstate Foundation
Allstate Plaza
CO6
Northbrook, IL 60062
(708) 402-5502

Description: Funding emphasis includes health and welfare, including youth organizations and community funds; funds children's hospitals in several states. Hospital funding most recently given in Florida, Colorado, Louisiana, District of Columbia, Illinois, Maryland, and Indiana.
Restrictions: N/A
$ Given: In 1989, 1,645 grants totaling $7,940,395; average range, $5,000 - $25,000
Application Information: Write for application guidelines; see the important information in the chapter introduction about the need for institutional affiliation.
Deadline: None
Contact: Fred Ramos, Executive Director

Thomas D. Buckley Trust
P.O. Box 647
Chappell, NE 69129
(308) 874-2212

Description: General purpose funding to hospitals and health services, as well as to other organizations.
Restrictions: Primary focus in Chappell, Nebraska and in Colorado
$ Given: In FY89, 58 grants totaling $266,736 were awarded; range of $250 - $35,000 per award; average range of $500 - $10,000 per award
Application Information: Write for application guidelines; see the important information in the chapter introduction about the need for institutional affiliation.
Deadline: None
Contact: Dwight E. Smith

Comprecare Foundation, Inc.
P.O. Box 441170
Aurora, CO 80044
(303) 322-1641

Description: "To encourage, aid or assist specific health related programs and to support the activities of organizations and individuals who advance and promote health care education, the delivery of health care services, and the improvement of community health and welfare"
Restrictions: Limited to Colorado
$ Given: In 1989, 16 grants totaling $215,066; range, $2,000 - $46,000
Application Information: Write for application guidelines; see the important information in the chapter introduction about the need for institutional affiliation.
Deadline: None
Contact: J.R. Gilsdorf, Executive Director

FLOW-THROUGH FUNDING

• •

Adolph Coors Foundation
350-C Clayton St.
Denver, CO 80206
(303) 388-1636

Description: Funding interests include human services, health, and youth.
Restrictions: Limited primarily to Colorado
$ Given: In FY89, 157 grants totaling $4,189,290; average range, $5,000 - $20,000
Application Information: Write for application guidelines; see the important information in the chapter introduction about the need for institutional affiliation.
Deadlines: February, May, August, and November
Contact: Linda S. Tafoya, Executive Director

Hasbro Children's Foundation

Description: (see full listing information under Alabama)

Keebler Company Foundation
One Hollow Tree Lane
Elmhurst, IL 60126
(312) 833-2900
APPLICATION ADDRESS:
677 Larch Ave.
Elmhurst, IL 60126

Description: Funding interests include minority programs, health and human services, and education.
Restrictions: Limited to Illinois, Colorado, Indiana, Michigan, Minnesota, North Carolina, Pennsylvania and Texas
$ Given: In 1987, 239 grants totaling $359,987; range, $10 - $34,180
Application Information: Write for application guidelines; see the important information in the chapter introduction about the need for institutional affiliation.
Deadline: None
Contact: A.G. Bland, Treasurer

US WEST Foundation

Description: (see full listing information under Arizona)

CONNECTICUT

Crestlea Foundation, Inc.
1004 Wilmington Trust Center
Wilmington, DE 19801

Description: Funding emphasis includes health agencies, higher and secondary education, social services, and youth agencies.
Restrictions: Limited to Connecticut and Delaware
$ Given: In 1988, 35 grants totaling $527,765; range, $500 - $225,565; average range, $1,000 - $25,000
Application Information: Write for application guidelines; see the important information in the chapter introduction about the need for institutional affiliation.
Deadline: N/A
Contact: Stewart E. Poole, President

Donaldson (Oliver S. and Jennie R.) Charitable Trust
c/o Durfee Attleboro Bank
Trust Department
Ten North Main St.
Fall River, MA 02720
(617) 679-8311

Description: Funding for such concerns as hospitals and health care agencies, child welfare and youth agencies, and cancer research and treatment programs.
Restrictions: Giving focused in the Northeast, with emphasis on Massachusetts; preference shown to 11 specific favored institutions
$ Given: In 1987, 37 grants totaling $858,440 were awarded; range of $1,680 - $68,000 per award
Application Information: Write for application guidelines; see the important information in the chapter introduction about the need for institutional affiliation.
Deadline: None; board meets quarterly to consider applications
Contact: William E. Murray, Chair of the Board of Trustees

Gimbel (Bernard F. and Alva B.) Foundation, Inc.
c/o Carol G. Lebworth
784 Park Ave.
New York, NY 10021
(212) 879-4119

Description: Funding for hospitals, hospices, rehabilitation programs, child welfare agencies, organizations for the disadvantaged, and other concerns.
Restrictions: Funding focused primarily in New York and Connecticut
$ Given: In 1988, 13 grants totaling $109,500 were awarded; range of $1,000 - $25,000 per award
Application Information: Write for application guidelines; see the important information in the chapter introduction about the need for institutional affiliation.
Deadline: None
Contact: Carol G. Lebworth, Co-President

Hagedorn Fund
c/o Manufacturers
Hanover Trust Company
270 Park Ave.
New York, NY 10017
(212) 270-9107

Description: General purpose funding for hospitals and health agencies, as well as for AIDS programs and many other organizations.
Restrictions: Limited to the New York City metropolitan area, including New Jersey and Connecticut
$ Given: In 1989, 114 grants totaling $1.1 million were awarded; range of $1,000 - $85,000 per award; average range of $5,000 - $10,000 per award
Application Information: Write for application guidelines; see the important information in the chapter introduction about the need for institutional affiliation.
Deadline: November 15
Contact: Robert Rosenthal, Vice President, Manufacturers Hanover Trust Company

FLOW-THROUGH FUNDING

• •

**Hasbro Children's
Foundation**

Description: (see full listing information under Alabama)

**J.M. McDonald
Foundation, Inc.**
2057 East River Rd.
Cortland, NY 13045-9752
(607) 756-9283

Description: General purpose funding for a variety of health-related concerns, including children who are ill, infirm, blind, crippled, and mentally or physically handicapped; funding to hospitals.
Restrictions: Funding focused in the Northeast
$ Given: In 1988, 26 grants totaling $405,000 were awarded; range of $2,500 - $30,000 per award; average range of $10,000 - $30,000 per award
Application Information: Write for application guidelines; see the important information in the chapter introduction about the need for institutional affiliation.
Deadlines: April 15, September 15
Contact: Reed L. McJunkin, Secretary

**The New Haven
Foundation**
One State St.
New Haven, CT 06510
(203) 777-2386

Description: Funding emphasis on social services, hospitals and health and youth agencies, including a resource center for older adolescents and their families.
Restrictions: Limited to greater New Haven and the lower Naugatuck River Valley, Connecticut
$ Given: In 1989, grants totaling $4,801,000
Application Information: Write for application guidelines; see the important information in the chapter introduction about the need for institutional affiliation.
Deadlines: January, April, August, and October
Contact: Helmer N. Ekstrom, Director

**The UPS Foundation,
Inc.**
Greenwich Office Park 5
Greenwich, CT 06836-3160
(203) 622-6201
(203) 622-6287

Description: Funding emphasis on programs for families and children in crisis, and health care.
Restrictions: No geographic restrictions
$ Given: In 1988, 202 grants totaling $6,112,174; average range, $2,000 - $50,000
Application Information: Write for application guidelines; see the important information in the chapter introduction about the need for institutional affiliation.
Deadline: January through August submissions preferred
Contact: Clement E. Hanrahan, Administrator

· ·

DELAWARE

Crestlea Foundation, Inc.
1004 Wilmington Trust Center
Wilmington, DE 19801

Description: Funding emphasis includes health agencies, higher and secondary education, social services, and youth agencies.
Restrictions: Limited to Connecticut and Delaware
$ Given: In 1988, 35 grants totaling $527,765; range, $500 - $225,565; average range, $1,000 - $25,000
Application Information: Write for application guidelines; see the important information in the chapter introduction about the need for institutional affiliation.
Deadline: N/A
Contact: Stewart E. Poole, President

Jesse Ball duPont Religious, Charitable and Educational Fund
225 Water St.
Suite 1200
Jacksonville, FL 32202-4424
(904) 353-0890

Description: Funding interests include health organizations and hospitals, including a clinic for newborn infants and their mothers in Gainesville, Florida.
Restrictions: Limited primarily to Florida, Delaware, and Virginia; limited to organizations receiving funds from the donor from 1960 to 1964
$ Given: In FY89, 109 grants totaling $5,034,391; average range, $5,000 - $100,000
Application Information: Write for application guidelines; see the important information in the chapter introduction about the need for institutional affiliation.
Deadline: None
Contact: George Penick, Executive Director

Hasbro Children's Foundation

Description: (see full listing information under Alabama)

DISTRICT OF COLUMBIA

The Allstate Foundation

Description: (see full listing information under Colorado)

FLOW-THROUGH FUNDING

• •

**The Cafritz (Morris
and Gwendolyn)
Foundation**
1825 K St., N.W.
14th Floor
Washington, DC 20006
(202) 223-3100

Description: Funds direct assistance programs, including a
lodging program for parents of chronically ill children during
treatment.
Restrictions: Limited to Washington, DC
$ Given: In FY89, 114 grants totaling $7,377,539; average range,
$10,000 - $50,000
Application Information: Write for application guidelines; see
the important information in the chapter introduction about the
need for institutional affiliation.
Deadlines: March 1, July 1, and November 1
Contact: Martin Atlas, President

CSG Foundation, Inc.
8401 Connecticut Ave.
Chevy Chase, MD 20815
(301) 652-6880

Description: Funding to organizations serving children.
Restrictions: Funding focused primarily in the Washington, DC area
$ Given: In 1988, 1 grant for $45,000 was awarded
Application Information: Write for application guidelines; see
the important information in the chapter introduction about the
need for institutional affiliation.
Deadline: None
Contact: W. Shepherdson Abell, Secretary-Treasurer

**Fannie Mae
Foundation**

Description: (see full listing information under California)

The Favrot Fund

Description: (see full listing information under California)

**Hasbro Children's
Foundation**

Description: (see full listing information under Alabama)

**The James M.
Johnston Trust for
Charitable and
Educational Purposes**
1101 Vermont Ave.,
N.W.
Suite 403
Washington, DC 20005
(202) 289-4996

Description: Funding interests include a hospital for sick children
Restrictions: Limited to Washington, DC, and North Carolina
$ Given: In 1988, 85 grants totaling $2,374,150; average range,
$10,000 - $30,000
Application Information: Write for application guidelines; see
the important information in the chapter introduction about the
need for institutional affiliation.
Deadline: None
Contact: Betty Frost Hayes, Chair

• •

George Preston Marshall Foundation
5454 Wisconsin Ave.
Suite 1455
Chevy Chase, MD 20815
(301) 654-7774

Description: Funding for providing health and welfare services to children.
Restrictions: Limited to Washington, DC, Maryland and Virginia
$ Given: In 1987, 68 grants totaling $414,640 were awarded; range of $325 - $27,000 per award
Application Information: Write for application guidelines; see the important information in the chapter introduction about the need for institutional affiliation.
Deadline: None
Contact: Elizabeth B. Frazier, Executive Director

Meyer (Eugene and Agnes E.) Foundation
1400 Sixteenth St., N.W.
Suite 360
Washington, DC 20036
(202) 483-8294

Description: Funding interests include health and mental health, including a center for maternal and child care.
Restrictions: Limited to the Washington, DC area, including Virginia and Maryland
$ Given: In 1989, 112 grants totaling $2,101,862; average range, $10,000 - $25,000
Application Information: Write for application guidelines; see the important information in the chapter introduction about the need for institutional affiliation.
Deadlines: April 1, August 1, and December 1
Contact: Julie L. Rogers, President

The Park Foundation
100 East 42nd St.
Suite 1850
New York, NY 10017

Description: General purpose funding for aid to the ill and infirm, including children, and for rehabilitation for the handicapped.
Restrictions: Funding focused primarily in New York, Massachusetts, and Washington, DC
$ Given: In 1988, grants totaling $184,400 were awarded
Application Information: Write for application guidelines; see the important information in the chapter introduction about the need for institutional affiliation.
Deadline: None
Contact: Richard S. Waite, Assistant Treasurer

FLOW-THROUGH FUNDING

• •

Public Welfare Foundation, Inc.
2600 Virginia Ave., N.W.
Room 505
Washington, DC 20037-1977
(202) 965-1800

Description: Funding interests include a pediatric health care clinic in Portland, Oregon and a youth health clinic in Elkins, Virginia.
Restrictions: No geographic restrictions
$ Given: In FY89, 341 grants totaling $12,331,100; range, $5,000 - $240,000; average, $36,000
Application Information: Write for application guidelines; see the important information in the chapter introduction about the need for institutional affiliation.
Deadline: None
Contact: C. Glenn Ihrig, Executive Director

RJR Nabisco Foundation
1455 Pennsylvania Ave., N.W.
Washington, DC 20004
(202) 626-7200

Description: Funding interests include a children's rehabilitation clinic in Atlanta, Georgia.
Restrictions: Guidelines currently being restructured
$ Given: In 1989, grants totaling $6,806,508; average range, $5,000 - $25,000
Application Information: Write for application guidelines; see the important information in the chapter introduction about the need for institutional affiliation.
Deadline: N/A
Contact: Jaynie M. Grant, Executive Director

FLORIDA

The Allstate Foundation

Description: (see full listing information under Colorado)

Edyth Bush Charitable Foundation, Inc.
199 East Wellbourne Ave.
P.O. Box 1967
Winter Park, FL 32790-1967
(407) 647-4322

Description: Funds charitable, educational, and health service organizations, with emphasis on human services and health.
Restrictions: Funding generally limited to within a one-hundred-mile radius of Winter Park, Florida
$ Given: In FY89, 58 grants totaling $2,260,296; range, $4,000 - $170,000; average range, $20,000 - $75,000
Application Information: Write for application guidelines; see the important information in the chapter introduction about the need for institutional affiliation.
Deadlines: September 1, January 1
Contact: H. Clifford Lee, President

**Conn Memorial
Foundation, Inc.**
220 East Madison St.
Suite 822
P.O. Box 229
Tampa, FL 33601
(813) 223-3838

Description: Funds health services and rehabilitation, as well as charities benefitting youth.
Restrictions: Limited to the greater Tampa Bay area of Florida
$ Given: In FY87, 49 grants totaling $778,220; range, $1,000 - $175,000; average range, $1,000 - $20,000
Application Information: Write for application guidelines; see the important information in the chapter introduction about the need for institutional affiliation.
Deadlines: November 30, May 31
Contact: David B. Frye, President

**Jesse Ball duPont
Religious, Charitable
and Educational Fund**

Description: (see full listing information under Delaware)

**Ralph Evinrude
Foundation, Inc.**
c/o Quarles and Brady
411 East Wisconsin Ave.
Milwaukee, WI 53202-4497
(414) 277-5000

Description: General and special purpose funding for hospitals, health agencies, mental health programs, services for the handicapped, and other social welfare organizations.
Restrictions: Limited primarily to Milwaukee, Wisconsin and Stuart, Florida
$ Given: In FY89, 53 grants totaling $131,750 were awarded; range of $350 - $25,000 per award; average range of $1,000 - $5,000 per award
Application Information: Write for application guidelines; see the important information in the chapter introduction about the need for institutional affiliation.
Deadline: Ongoing; January, April, July, and October submissions preferred
Contact: Patrick W. Cotter, Vice President

**Charles A. Frueauff
Foundation, Inc.**
306 East Seventh Ave.
Tallahassee, FL 32303
(904) 561-3508

Description: Areas of support include hospitals, mental health and other health services.
Restrictions: No geographic restrictions
$ Given: In 1988, 195 grants totaling $2,824,500; range, $1,500 - $50,000
Application Information: Write for application guidelines; see the important information in the chapter introduction about the need for institutional affiliation.
Deadline: March 15
Contact: David A. Frueauff, Secretary

• • • • • • • • • • • • • • • • • • •

Hasbro Children's Foundation

Description: (see full listing information under Alabama)

Lost Tree Charitable Foundation, Inc.
11555 Lost Tree Way
North Palm Beach, FL
33408
(407) 622-3780

Description: Funding interests include education and health services
Restrictions: Limited to Palm Beach and Martin counties, Florida
$ Given: In 1989, 30 grants totaling $146,354; range, $500 - $14,500
Application Information: Write for application guidelines; see the important information in the chapter introduction about the need for institutional affiliation.
Deadline: None
Contact: Robert C. Porter, President, or Pamela M. Rue, Executive Secretary

D.W. McMillan Foundation

Description: (see full listing information under Alabama)

Monsanto Fund

Description: (see full listing information under Alabama)

GEORGIA

J. Bulow Campbell Foundation
1401 Trust Company
Tower
25 Park Place, N.E.
Atlanta, GA 30303
(404) 658-9066

Description: Supports education, youth development and health, including a treatment center in Atlanta, Georgia.
Restrictions: Grants given primarily in Georgia
$ Given: In 1989, 30 grants totaling $6,348,970; range, $25,000 - $500,000; average range, $100,000 - $200,000
Application Information: Write for application guidelines; see the important information in the chapter introduction about the need for institutional affiliation.
Deadlines: January 15, April 15, July 15, and October 15
Contact: John W. Stephenson, Executive Director

The Coca-Cola Foundation, Inc.

Description: (see full listing information under California)

Fannie Mae Foundation

Description: (see full listing information under California)

E.J. Grassman Trust
P.O. Box 4470
Warren, NJ 07060
(201) 753-2440

Description: Funding for a wide variety of concerns, including hospitals, health organizations, and child welfare agencies.
Restrictions: Funding limited primarily to Union County, New Jersey, and to middle Georgia
$ Given: In 1989, 154 grants totaling $2.24 million were awarded; range of $1,500 - $145,000 per award; average range of $5,000 - $30,000 per award
Application Information: Write for application guidelines; see the important information in the chapter introduction about the need for institutional affiliation.
Deadlines: April 20, October 15
Contact: William V. Engel, Executive Director

Hasbro Children's Foundation

Description: (see full listing information under Alabama)

Levi Strauss Foundation

Description: (see full listing information under Arkansas)

Metropolitan Atlanta Community Foundation, Inc.
The Hurt Building
Suite 449
Atlanta, GA 30303
(404) 688-5525

Description: Funding interests include health and social services, including a children's hospital in Atlanta, Georgia.
Restrictions: Limited to the metropolitan area of Atlanta, Georgia
$ Given: In FY89, 442 grants totaling $5,191,270; average range, $3,000 - $5,000
Application Information: Write for application guidelines; see the important information in the chapter introduction about the need for institutional affiliation.
Deadlines: March 15, September 15, and November 15
Contact: Alicia Philipps, Executive Director

Monsanto Fund

Description: (see full listing information under Alabama)

RJR Nabisco Foundation

Description: (see full listing information under District of Columbia)

FLOW-THROUGH FUNDING

. . . .

HAWAII

**First Hawaiian
Foundation**
165 South King St.
Honolulu, HI 96813
(808) 525-8144

Description: Funds social services, health services, education, and a community fund.
Restrictions: Limited to Hawaii
$ Given: In 1988, 50 grants totaling $733,536; range, $177 - $127,000; average range, $500 - $100,000
Application Information: Write for application guidelines; see the important information in the chapter introduction about the need for institutional affiliation.
Deadline: None
Contact: Herbert E. Wolff, Secretary

**Hasbro Children's
Foundation**

Description: (see full listing information under Alabama)

**Hawaiian Electric
Industries Charitable
Foundation**
P.O. Box 730
Honolulu, HI 96808
(808) 543-7356

Description: Funding interests include health, hospitals, and community development.
Restrictions: Limited primarily to Hawaii
$ Given: In 1989, 201 grants totaling $812,000; range, $300 - $25,000
Application Information: Write for application guidelines; see the important information in the chapter introduction about the need for institutional affiliation.
Deadlines: December 1, June 1
Contact: Ted Souza

IDAHO

**The Dumke (Dr.
Ezekiel R. and Edna
Wattis) Foundation**
600 Crandall Building
Ten West First South
Salt Lake City, UT
84101
(801) 363-7863

Description: General purpose and special project funding for medical and hospital services, as well as for other concerns.
Restrictions: Funding focused primarily in Utah and Idaho
$ Given: In 1988, 27 grants totaling $262,000 were awarded; range of $1,000 - $40,000 per award
Application Information: Write for application guidelines; see the important information in the chapter introduction about the need for institutional affiliation.
Deadlines: February 1, July1
Contact: Max B. Lewis, Secretary

**Hasbro Children's
Foundation**

Description: (see full listing information under Alabama)

George Frederick Jewett Foundation
One Maritime Plaza
Suite 990
San Francisco, CA
94111
(415) 421-1351

Description: General and special purpose funding to address a wide variety of human welfare concerns, including funding for health care and medical services.
Restrictions: Funding focused primarily in the Pacific Northwest, especially in northern Idaho, eastern Washington (with emphasis on Spokane), and San Francisco, California
$ Given: In 1989, 134 grants totaling $953,600 were awarded; range of $500 - $25,000 per award; average range of $1,000 - $15,000 per award
Application Information: Write for application guidelines; see the important information in the chapter introduction about the need for institutional affiliation.
Deadlines: February 15, May 15, August 15, and November 1
Contact: Theresa A. Mullen, Program Director

Meyer Memorial Trust

Description: (see full listing information under Alaska)

Monsanto Fund

Description: (see full listing information under Alabama)

US WEST Foundation

Description: (see full listing information under Arizona)

ILLINOIS

The Allstate Foundation

Description: (see full listing information under Colorado)

The Barker Welfare Foundation
One First National Plaza
Suite 2544
Chicago, IL 60603
(516) 759-5592

Description: General funding to established organizations, including health service agencies, rehabilitation centers, handicapped services organizations, etc.
Restrictions: Limited to New York City; Chicago, Illinois; and Michigan City, Indiana
$ Given: In FY89, 200 grants totaling $1.58 million were awarded; range of $1,000 - $50,000 per award; average range of $3,000 - $9,000 per award
Application Information: Write for application guidelines; see the important information in the chapter introduction about the need for institutional affiliation.
Deadline: February 1
Contact: Philip D. Block III

FLOW-THROUGH FUNDING

• • • • • • • • • • • • • • • • • • • •

The Blum (Nathan and Emily S.) Fund
111 West Monroe St.
Chicago, IL 60603
(312) 461-2613
APPLICATION ADDRESS:
c/o Harris Bank
P.O. Box 755
Chicago, IL 60690

Description: Funds hospitals, health and social service agencies, and Jewish welfare funds.
Restrictions: Limited to Chicago, Illinois
$ Given: In 1988, 10 grants totaling $360,000; range, $2,000 - $102,000
Application Information: Write for application guidelines; see the important information in the chapter introduction about the need for institutional affiliation.
Deadline: None
Contact: Ellen A. Bechtold, Vice President, Harris Trust and Savings Bank

Borg-Warner Foundation, Inc.
200 South Michigan Ave.
Chicago, IL 60604
(312) 322-8659

Description: Funding interests include community funds, social welfare, and health services
Restrictions: Limited primarily to the Chicago, Illinois area
$ Given: In 1988, 150 grants totaling $1,295,455; range, $500 - $200,000; average range, $2,500 - $10,000
Application Information: Write for application guidelines; see the important information in the chapter introduction about the need for institutional affiliation.
Deadline: March 1 (letter of intent); May 1 (proposal)
Contact: Ellen J. Benjamin, Director of Corporate Contributions

Crown (Arie and Ida) Memorial
222 North LaSalle St.
Chicago, IL 60601
(312) 236-6300

Description: Funding interests include youth agencies and health care, including Children's Memorial Hospital and the Infant Welfare Society, in Chicago, Illinois.
Restrictions: Limited to the Chicago, Illinois area
$ Given: In 1988, grants totaling $3,765,850; average range, $100 - $25,000
Application Information: Write for application guidelines; see the important information in the chapter introduction about the need for institutional affiliation.
Deadlines: January 30, May 31, and September 30
Contact: Susan Crown, President

John Deere Foundation
John Deere Rd.
Moline, IL 61265
(309) 765-4137

Description: Areas of support include health services, community funds, youth agencies, and education
Restrictions: Limited to Iowa, Illinois, and Wisconsin
$ Given: In FY89, grants totaling $3,707,974; range, $500 - $539,500; average range, $500 - $5,000
Application Information: Write for application guidelines; see the important information in the chapter introduction about the need for institutional affiliation.
Deadline: None
Contact: Donald R. Margenthaler, President

The Donaldson Foundation
c/o Donaldson Company, Inc.
P.O. Box 1299
Minneapolis, MN 55440
(612) 887-3010

Description: Funding interests include health services, environmental protection, and higher education
Restrictions: Limited to Illinois, Indiana, Iowa, Kentucky, Minnesota, Missouri, and Wisconsin
$ Given: In FY88, 98 grants totaling $338,875; range, $300 - $38,400
Application Information: Write for application guidelines; see the important information in the chapter introduction about the need for institutional affiliation.
Deadlines: May 1, August 1
Contact: Raymond Vodovnik, Secretary

Fannie Mae Foundation

Description: (see full listing information under California)

Frankel Foundation
c/o Harris Trust & Savings Bank
111 West Monroe St.
Chicago, IL 60603
APPLICATION ADDRESS:
P.O. Box 755
Chicago, IL 60603

Description: Funding interests include hospitals and social services, including children's hospitals.
Restrictions: Limited to Illinois
$ Given: In FY88, 37 grants totaling $1,655,500; range, $3,000 - $530,000
Application Information: Write for application guidelines; see the important information in the chapter introduction about the need for institutional affiliation.
Deadline: None
Contact: Ellen A. Bechtold

Hasbro Children's Foundation

Description: (see full listing information under Alabama)

FLOW-THROUGH FUNDING

• •

Iowa and Illinois Gas and Electric Company Giving Program
206 East Second St.
Davenport, IA 52802
(319) 326-7038

Description: Areas of support include health care, child welfare, and hospitals and health services
Restrictions: Limited to Davenport, Bettendorf, Cedar Rapids, Iowa City, and Fort Dodge, Iowa; Rock Island and Moline, Illinois; and Ohio
$ Given: In 1987, 186 grants totaling $ 537,065; range, $10 - $106,375
Application Information: Write for application guidelines; see the important information in the chapter introduction about the need for institutional affiliation.
Deadline: None
Contact: J.C. Decker, Secretary-Treasurer

Keebler Company Foundation

Description: (see full listing information under Colorado)

Kraft General Foods Foundation
Kraft Court
Glenview, IL 60025
(708) 998-7032

Description: Support for self-help programs, with emphasis on the needs of minorities, people with disabilities, and women; funds La Rabida Children's Hospital and Research Center in Chicago, Illinois
Restrictions: Funds programs with national impact and programs in areas of company representation
$ Given: In 1988, grants totaling $10,467,690; average range, $25,000 - $50,000
Application Information: Write for application guidelines; see the important information in the chapter introduction about the need for institutional affiliation.
Deadline: None
Contact: Ronald J. Coman, Administrative Director

Material Service Foundation
222 North LaSalle St.
Chicago, IL 60601

Description: Funding interests include health services and community development.
Restrictions: Limited to Illinois, with emphasis on Chicago
$ Given: In 1989, 139 grants totaling $283,100; range, $25 - $100,000; average range, $1,000 - $2,000
Application Information: Write for application guidelines; see the important information in the chapter introduction about the need for institutional affiliation.
Deadline: None
Contact: Louis J. Levy, Administrator

Robert R. McCormick Charitable Trust
435 North Michigan Ave.
Suite 770
Chicago, IL 60611
(312) 222-3510

Description: Funding interests include health services, family and legal services, women, and youth, including a teen health program and a pediatric dental clinic.
Restrictions: Limited to the Chicago, Illinois metropolitan area
$ Given: In 1989, 427 grants totaling $19,904,476; average range, $2,500 - $100,000
Application Information: Write for application guidelines; see the important information in the chapter introduction about the need for institutional affiliation.
Deadlines: February 1, May 1, August 1, and November 1
Contact: Claude A. Smith, Director of Philanthropy

Monsanto Fund

Description: (see full listing information under Alabama)

The Northern Trust Company Charitable Trust
c/o The Northern Trust Company
50 South LaSalle St.
Chicago, IL 60675
(312) 444-3538

Description: Funding interests include health services, hospitals and social services
Restrictions: Limited to the metropolitan Chicago, Illinois area
$ Given: In 1988, 645 grants totaling $1,182,538; range, $25 - $154,000; average range, $2,000 - $5,000
Application Information: Write for application guidelines; see the important information in the chapter introduction about the need for institutional affiliation.
Deadline: February 1
Contact: Marjorie W. Lundy, Vice President, The Northern Trust Company

Prince Charitable Trusts
Ten South Wacker Drive
Suite 2575
Chicago, IL 60606
(312) 454-9130

Description: Funding interests include youth organizations, social services, and hospitals.
Restrictions: Limited to Chicago, Illinois and Rhode Island
$ Given: In 1988, grants totaling $3,623,507; average range, $5,000 - $25,000
Application Information: Write for application guidelines; see the important information in the chapter introduction about the need for institutional affiliation.
Deadline: None
Contact: N/A

FLOW-THROUGH FUNDING

• •

Dr. Scholl Foundation
11 South LaSalle St.
Suite 2100
Chicago, IL 60603
(312) 782-5210

Description: Supports programs for children, grants to hospitals, and medical and nursing institutions, including a community nursing service in Salt Lake City, Utah.
Restrictions: No geographic limitations
$ Given: In 1989, 372 grants totaling $7,371,300; range, $1,000 - $200,000; average range, $5,000 - $50,000
Application Information: Write for application guidelines; see the important information in the chapter introduction about the need for institutional affiliation.
Deadline: May 15
Contact: Jack E. Scholl, Executive Director

**The Otho S.A.
Sprague Memorial
Institute**
c/o Harris Trust and
Savings Bank
190 South LaSalle St.
Fourth Floor
Chicago, IL 60690
(312) 461-7054

Description: Funding interests include the prevention and relief of human suffering caused by disease.
Restrictions: Limited to Chicago, Illinois
$ Given: In 1988, five grants totaling $600,000; range, $15,000 - $190,000
Application Information: Write for application guidelines; see the important information in the chapter introduction about the need for institutional affiliation.
Deadline: None
Contact: Thomas E. Macior

**Sundstrand
Corporation Foundation**
4949 Harrison Ave.
P.O. Box 7003
Rockford, IL 61125
(815) 226-6000

Description: Areas of support include community funds, education, and social and health services, including a children's hospital in Milwaukee, Wisconsin.
Restrictions: Limited to areas of company operations
$ Given: In FY88, 112 grants totaling $845,850; range, $450 - $122,000
Application Information: Write for application guidelines; see the important information in the chapter introduction about the need for institutional affiliation.
Deadline: None
Contact: Clarice Kieselburg, Secretary

Woods Charitable Fund, Inc.
Three First National Plaza
Suite 2010
Chicago, IL 60602
(312) 782-2698

Description: Funding interests include health clinics, including Sniffles, a children's clinic for the mildly ill, and Healy Mothers and Babies Coalition, both in Chicago, Illinois.
Restrictions: Limited to Chicago, Illinois, and Lincoln, Nebraska areas
$ Given: In 1989, 185 grants totaling $2,285,807; average range, $10,000 - $20,000
Application Information: Write for application guidelines; see the important information in the chapter introduction about the need for institutional affiliation.
Deadlines: April 15, July 15, and October 15
Contact: Jean Rudd, Executive Director

INDIANA

The Allstate Foundation
Description: (see full listing information under Colorado)

The Barker Welfare Foundation
Description: (see full listing information under Illinois)

The Donaldson Foundation
Description: (see full listing information under Illinois)

Hasbro Children's Foundation
Description: (see full listing information under Alabama)

Keebler Company Foundation
Description: (see full listing information under Colorado)

IOWA

John Deere Foundation
Description: (see full listing information under Illinois)

The Donaldson Foundation
Description: (see full listing information under Illinois)

FLOW-THROUGH FUNDING

. . . .

The Hall Foundation, Inc.
115 Third St. S.E.
No. 803
Cedar Rapids, IA 52401
(319) 362-9079

Description: Funding interests include youth agencies, hospitals, and health services.
Restrictions: Limited to Cedar Rapids, Iowa, and the immediate area
$ Given: In 1989, 35 grants totaling $3,395,564; range, $500 - $680,000; average range, $5,000 - $100,000
Application Information: Write for application guidelines; see the important information in the chapter introduction about the need for institutional affiliation.
Deadline: None
Contact: John G. Lidvall, Executive Director

Hasbro Children's Foundation

Description: (see full listing information under Alabama)

Iowa and Illinois Gas and Electric Company Giving Program

Description: (see full listing information under Illinois)

Mid-Iowa Health Foundation
550 39th St.
Suite 104
Des Moines, IA 50312
(515) 277-6411

Description: Funds health-related service projects including drug abuse, mental health, and nutrition.
Restrictions: Limited to Polk County, Iowa, and seven surrounding counties
$ Given: In 1988, 41 grants totaling $459,129; range, $700 - $27,345; average range, $1,000 - $50,000
Application Information: Write for application guidelines; see the important information in the chapter introduction about the need for institutional affiliation.
Deadlines: February 1, May 1, August 1, and November 1
Contact: Kathryn Bradley

US WEST Foundation

Description: (see full listing information under Arizona)

KANSAS

Hasbro Children's Foundation

Description: (see full listing information under Alabama)

• • • • • • • • • • • • • • • • • • • •

**Ewing Marion
Kauffman Foundation**
922 Walnut St.
Suite 1100
Kansas City, MO 64106
(816) 966-4000
APPLICATION ADDRESS:
9300 Ward Parkway
P.O. Box 8480
Kansas City, MO 64114

Description: Funding focused on health agencies, with additional giving for other concerns.
Restrictions: Limited to Kansas and Missouri. Most funds are disbursed through programs directly administered by the foundation itself; few outright grants are awarded.
$ Given: In FY89, 20 grants totaling $201,639 were awarded; range of $50 - $75,000 per award; plus $478,000 in support for foundation-administered programs
Application Information: Write for application guidelines; see the important information in the chapter introduction about the need for institutional affiliation.
Deadline: None
Contact: Carl Mitchell, Treasurer

**Rice (Ethel and
Raymond F.)
Foundation**
700 Massachusetts St.
Lawrence, KS 66044
(913) 843-0420

Description: Areas of support include education, health, youth and social service agencies
Restrictions: Limited to the Lawrence, Kansas area
$ Given: In 1987, 80 grants totaling $235,885; range, $500 - $16,000
Application Information: Write for application guidelines; see the important information in the chapter introduction about the need for institutional affiliation.
Deadline: November 15
Contact: Robert B. Oyler, President, or George M. Klem, Treasurer

**Speas (John W. and
Effie E.) Memorial
Trust**
c/o Boatmen's First
National Bank of
Kansas City
14 West Tenth St.
Kansas City, MO 64183
(816) 691-7481
APPLICATION ADDRESS:
Boatmen's First
National Bank of
Kansas City
P.O. Box 419038
Kansas City, MO 64183

Description: General and special project funding to hospitals and health services, including support for the mentally disabled.
Restrictions: Limited to the greater metropolitan Kansas City area
$ Given: In 1989, 28 grants totaling $1.19 million were awarded; range of $5,000 - $152,000 per award; average range of $5,000 - $100,000 per award
Application Information: Write for application guidelines; see the important information in the chapter introduction about the need for institutional affiliation.
Deadline: None
Contact: David P. Ross, Senior Vice President, Boatmen's First National Bank of Kansas City

FLOW-THROUGH FUNDING

• •

KENTUCKY

James Graham Brown Foundation, Inc.
132 East Gray St.
Louisville, KY 40202
(502) 583-4085

Description: Funding interests include community development, health services, and youth.
Restrictions: Limited to Kentucky, with emphasis on Louisville
$ Given: In 1989, 60 grants totaling $8,459,687; range, $100 - $1,500,000; average range, $5,000 - $250,000
Application Information: Write for application guidelines; see the important information in the chapter introduction about the need for institutional affiliation.
Deadline: None
Contact: Mason Rummel, Grants Coordinator

The Cralle Foundation
c/o Liberty National
Bank & Trust Company
of Louisville
P.O. Box 32500
Louisville, KY 40232
(502) 566-1702

Description: Funds education, health services, youth groups, and community development.
Restrictions: Limited to Kentucky, with emphasis on Louisville
$ Given: In 1988, 18 grants totaling $785,833; range, $3,500 - $300,000
Application Information: Write for application guidelines; see the important information in the chapter introduction about the need for institutional affiliation.
Deadlines: None
Contact: Institutional Trust Department

The Donaldson Foundation

Description: (see full listing information under Illinois)

The Gheens Foundation, Inc.
One Riverfront Plaza
Suite 705
Louisville, KY 40202
(502) 584-4650

Description: Some emphasis on programs for the physically handicapped, including a pre-school vision screening program in Louisville, Kentucky.
Restrictions: Limited primarily to Kentucky, with emphasis on Louisville
$ Given: In FY88, 54 grants totaling $1,295,274; average range, $5,000 - $50,000
Application Information: Write for application guidelines; see the important information in the chapter introduction about the need for institutional affiliation.
Deadline: None
Contact: James N. Davis, Executive Director

• • • • • • • • • • • • • • • • • • • •

Hasbro Children's Foundation

Description: (see full listing information under Alabama)

Levi Strauss Foundation

Description: (see full listing information under Arkansas)

LOUISIANA

The Allstate Foundation

Description: (see full listing information under Colorado)

The Community Foundation of Shreveport-Bossier
401 Edwards St.
Suite 1520
Shreveport, LA 71101
(318) 221-0582

Description: Funds health services, education, and youth agencies
Restrictions: Limited to Caddo and Bossier parishes, Louisiana
$ Given: In 1988, 41 grants totaling $691,920; range, $170 - $100,000
Application Information: Write for application guidelines; see the important information in the chapter introduction about the need for institutional affiliation.
Deadlines: March 1, June 1, September 1
Contact: Carol Emanuel, Executive Director

German Protestant Orphan Asylum Association
5342 St. Charles Ave.
New Orleans, LA 70115
(504) 895-2361

Description: Areas of support include medical services, child welfare, family services, and youth programs
Restrictions: Limited to Louisiana
$ Given: In FY89, 18 grants totaling $227,194; range, $1,980 - $35,931
Application Information: Write for application guidelines; see the important information in the chapter introduction about the need for institutional affiliation.
Deadlines: December, March, June, and September
Contact: Everett T. Aultman, Executive Director

FLOW-THROUGH FUNDING

Speas (John W. and Effie E.) Memorial Trust
c/o Boatmen's First National Bank of Kansas City
14 West Tenth St.
Kansas City, MO 64183
(816) 691-7481
APPLICATION ADDRESS:
Boatmen's First National Bank of Kansas City
P.O. Box 419038
Kansas City, MO 64183

Description: General and special project funding to hospitals and health services, including support for the mentally disabled.
Restrictions: Limited to the greater metropolitan Kansas City area
$ Given: In 1989, 28 grants totaling $1.19 million were awarded; range of $5,000 - $152,000 per award; average range of $5,000 - $100,000 per award
Application Information: Write for application guidelines; see the important information in the chapter introduction about the need for institutional affiliation.
Deadline: None
Contact: David P. Ross, Senior Vice President, Boatmen's First National Bank of Kansas City

KENTUCKY

James Graham Brown Foundation, Inc.
132 East Gray St.
Louisville, KY 40202
(502) 583-4085

Description: Funding interests include community development, health services, and youth.
Restrictions: Limited to Kentucky, with emphasis on Louisville
$ Given: In 1989, 60 grants totaling $8,459,687; range, $100 - $1,500,000; average range, $5,000 - $250,000
Application Information: Write for application guidelines; see the important information in the chapter introduction about the need for institutional affiliation.
Deadline: None
Contact: Mason Rummel, Grants Coordinator

The Cralle Foundation
c/o Liberty National Bank & Trust Company of Louisville
P.O. Box 32500
Louisville, KY 40232
(502) 566-1702

Description: Funds education, health services, youth groups, and community development.
Restrictions: Limited to Kentucky, with emphasis on Louisville
$ Given: In 1988, 18 grants totaling $785,833; range, $3,500 - $300,000
Application Information: Write for application guidelines; see the important information in the chapter introduction about the need for institutional affiliation.
Deadlines: None
Contact: Institutional Trust Department

• • • • • • • • • • • • • • • • • • • •

**The Donaldson
Foundation**

Description: (see full listing information under Illinois)

**The Gheens
Foundation, Inc.**
One Riverfront Plaza
Suite 705
Louisville, KY 40202
(502) 584-4650

Description: Some emphasis on programs for the physically
handicapped, including a pre-school vision screening program in
Louisville, Kentucky.
Restrictions: Limited primarily to Kentucky, with emphasis on
Louisville
$ Given: In FY88, 54 grants totaling $1,295,274; average range,
$5,000 - $50,000
Application Information: Write for application guidelines; see
the important information in the chapter introduction about the
need for institutional affiliation.
Deadline: None
Contact: James N. Davis, Executive Director

**Hasbro Children's
Foundation**

Description: (see full listing information under Alabama)

**Levi Strauss
Foundation**

Description: (see full listing information under Arkansas)

LOUISIANA

The Allstate Foundation

Description: (see full listing information under Colorado)

**The Community
Foundation of
Shreveport-Bossier**
401 Edwards St.
Suite 1520
Shreveport, LA 71101
(318) 221-0582

Description: Funds health services, education, and youth agencies
Restrictions: Limited to Caddo and Bossier parishes, Louisiana
$ Given: In 1988, 41 grants totaling $691,920; range, $170 -
$100,000
Application Information: Write for application guidelines; see
the important information in the chapter introduction about the
need for institutional affiliation.
Deadlines: March 1, June 1, September 1
Contact: Carol Emanuel, Executive Director

FLOW-THROUGH FUNDING

• •

German Protestant Orphan Asylum Association
5342 St. Charles Ave.
New Orleans, LA 70115
(504) 895-2361

Description: Areas of support include medical services, child welfare, family services, and youth programs
Restrictions: Limited to Louisiana
$ Given: In FY89, 18 grants totaling $227,194; range, $1,980 - $35,931
Application Information: Write for application guidelines; see the important information in the chapter introduction about the need for institutional affiliation.
Deadlines: December, March, June, and September
Contact: Everett T. Aultman, Executive Director

Goldring Family Foundation
809 Jefferson Highway
Jefferson, LA 70121

Description: Funding interests include health services and community funds, with emphasis on Jewish welfare and education.
Restrictions: Limited to Louisiana
$ Given: In FY88, 29 grants totaling $384,640; range, $100 - $200,000
Application Information: Write for application guidelines; see the important information in the chapter introduction about the need for institutional affiliation.
Deadline: None
Contact: Stephen Goldring, President

Hasbro Children's Foundation

Description: (see full listing information under Alabama)

MAINE

Foundation for Seacoast Health
P.O. Box 4606
Portsmouth, NH 03801
(603) 433-4001

Description: Support for health care in five areas, two of which are "infants/children" and "adolescents."
Restrictions: Limited to Portsmouth, Rye, New Castle, Greenland, Newington, and North Hampton, New Hampshire; and to Kittery, Eliot and York, Maine
$ Given: In 1989, 39 grants totaling $634,800 were awarded; range of $500 - $125,000 per award
Application Information: Write for application guidelines; see the important information in the chapter introduction about the need for institutional affiliation.
Deadlines: March 1 for infants/children; June 1 for adolescents
Contact: Rodney G. Brock, President

Hasbro Children's Foundation

Description: (see full listing information under Alabama)

• • • • • • • • • • • • • • • • • • • •

Kenduskeag Foundation
c/o Dead River Company
One Dana St.
Portland, ME 04101
(207) 773-5841

Description: Funding for hospitals and other local charities for annual campaigns and special projects.
Restrictions: Limited to Maine
$ Given: In 1988, 11 grants totaling $65,933 were awarded; range of $350 - $30,000 per award
Application Information: Write for application guidelines; see the important information in the chapter introduction about the need for institutional affiliation.
Deadline: None
Contact: P. Andrews Nixon, Trustee

Agnes M. Lindsay Trust
45 Market St.
Manchester, NH 03101
(603) 669-4140

Description: General funding focused on child welfare and health services, as well as services for the handicapped.
Restrictions: Limited to Maine, Massachusetts, New Hampshire, and Vermont
$ Given: In 1988, 191 grants totaling $863,771 were awarded; range of $1,000 - $10,000 per award
Application Information: Write for application guidelines; see the important information in the chapter introduction about the need for institutional affiliation.
Deadline: Proposals considered monthly
Contact: Robert L. Chiesa, Trustee

J.M. McDonald Foundation, Inc.

Description: (see full listing information under Connecticut)

MARYLAND

The Allstate Foundation

Description: (see full listing information under Colorado)

The Blaustein (Louis and Henrietta) Foundation, Inc.
Blaustein Bldg.
P.O. Box 238
Baltimore, MD 21203

Description: General funding to established recipients, including local hospitals and health services providers.
Restrictions: Funding focused primarily in the Baltimore metropolitan area
$ Given: In 1988, 29 grants totaling $773,185 were awarded; range of $500 - $360,485 per award
Application Information: Write for application guidelines; see the important information in the chapter introduction about the need for institutional affiliation.
Deadline: None
Contact: Morton K. Blaustein, President

FLOW-THROUGH FUNDING

• • • • • • • • • • • • • • • • • • • •

Donaldson (Oliver S. and Jennie R.) Charitable Trust
c/o Durfee Attleboro Bank
Trust Department
Ten North Main St.
Fall River, MA 02720
(617) 679-8311

Description: Funding for such concerns as hospitals and health care agencies, child welfare and youth agencies, and cancer research and treatment programs.
Restrictions: Giving focused in the Northeast, with emphasis on Massachusetts; preference shown to 11 specific favored institutions
$ Given: In 1987, 37 grants totaling $858,440 were awarded; range of $1,680 - $68,000 per award
Application Information: Write for application guidelines; see the important information in the chapter introduction about the need for institutional affiliation.
Deadline: None; board meets quarterly to consider applications
Contact: William E. Murray, Chair of the Board of Trustees

Hasbro Children's Foundation

Description: (see full listing information under Alabama)

The Hopedale Foundation
43 Hope St.
Hopedale, MA 01747
(508) 473-0820

Description: Funding to local hospitals and other organizations. New grants given only where a direct impact on the local community can be demonstrated.
Restrictions: Limited primarily to Massachusetts
$ Given: In FY89, 22 grants totaling $163,433 were awarded; range of $1,500 - $55,000 per award
Application Information: Write for application guidelines; see the important information in the chapter introduction about the need for institutional affiliation.
Deadline: None
Contact: Thad R. Jackson, Treasurer

Agnes M. Lindsay Trust

Description: (see full listing information under Maine)

J.M. McDonald Foundation, Inc.

Description: (see full listing information under Connecticut)

Monsanto Fund

Description: (see full listing information under Alabama)

The Park Foundation

Description: (see full listing information under District of Columbia)

Edwin Phillips Trust
c/o Bank of New
England, N.A.
28 State St.
Boston, MA 02107
APPLICATION ADDRESS:
147 Bay State Rd.
Boston, MA 02215
(617) 353-2200

Description: Funding to organizations providing services to or performing research concerning physically or mentally ill children.
Restrictions: Funding focused primarily in Plymouth County, Massachusetts
$ Given: In 1988, 11 grants totaling $366,000 were awarded; range of $7,500 - $75,000 per award
Application Information: Write for application guidelines; see the important information in the chapter introduction about the need for institutional affiliation.
Deadline: N/A
Contact: Jon Westling, Assistant to the President, Boston University

Rubenstein (Lawrence J. and Anne) Charitable Foundation
Beacon Hill Capitol
Corporation
84 State St.
No. 700
Boston, MA 02109

Description: General funding for hospitals and other institutions, with emphasis on medical care and research of children's illnesses.
Restrictions: Limited primarily to Massachusetts
$ Given: In FY87, grants totaling $500,000 were awarded; range of $10,000 - $350,000 per award
Application Information: Write for application guidelines; see the important information in the chapter introduction about the need for institutional affiliation.
Deadline: May 1
Contact: Richard I. Kaner, Trustee

MICHIGAN

A.G. Bishop Charitable Trust
c/o NBD Genesee
Merchants Bank & Trust
Company
One East First St.
Flint, MI 48502
(313) 766-8307

Description: Funding for a specified hospital and various health care agencies, as well as for other organizations.
Restrictions: Strictly limited to the community of Flint-Genesee County, Michigan
$ Given: In 1988, 49 grants totaling $227,837 were awarded; range of $750 - $33,300 per award
Application Information: Write for application guidelines; see the important information in the chapter introduction about the need for institutional affiliation.
Deadline: None
Contact: C. Ann Barton, Trust Officer

FLOW-THROUGH FUNDING

• •

**Carls (William &
Marie) Foundation**
100 Renaissance Center
Suite 1880
Detroit, MI 48243-1062
(313) 259-3070

Description: Funding to medical and recreational facilities serving handicapped or underprivileged children.
Restrictions: N/A
$ Given: In 1988, 6 grants totaling $174,425 were awarded; range of $1,000 - $123,000 per award
Application Information: Write for application guidelines; see the important information in the chapter introduction about the need for institutional affiliation.
Deadline: None
Contact: Harold Stieg, Vice President

**Hasbro Children's
Foundation**

Description: (see full listing information under Alabama)

Herrick Foundation
2500 Comerica Building
Detroit, MI 48226
(313) 963-6420

Description: Funding for hospitals, as well as for a wide variety of other organizations.
Restrictions: Primary focus on Michigan
$ Given: In FY88, 190 grants totaling $10.7 million were awarded; range of $500 - $1 million per award; average range of $5,000 - $100,000 per award
Application Information: Write for application guidelines; see the important information in the chapter introduction about the need for institutional affiliation.
Deadline: None
Contact: Kenneth G. Herrick, President

**Keebler Company
Foundation**

Description: (see full listing information under Colorado)

**Milan (Charles &
Florence) Foundation**
16500 North Park Drive
Apartment 1708
Southfield, MI 48075

Description: Funding for Jewish organizations and health services, including those for children.
Restrictions: N/A
$ Given: In FY88, 1 grant for $105,000 was awarded
Application Information: Write for application guidelines; see the important information in the chapter introduction about the need for institutional affiliation.
Deadline: N/A
Contact: Charles Milan, President

• • • • • • • • • • • • • • • • • • • •

Monsanto Fund

Description: (see full listing information under Alabama)

Pagel (William M. and Mary E.) Trust
c/o National Bank of Detroit
611 Woodward Ave.
Detroit, MI 48226
(313) 225-3124
APPLICATION ADDRESS:
c/o National Bank of Detroit
P.O. Box 222
Detroit, MI 48232

Description: General purpose funding for hospitals, health services, child welfare, rehabilitation, aid to the handicapped, etc.
Restrictions: Limited primarily to Michigan, with emphasis on the three counties of the Detroit metropolitan area
$ Given: In 1989, 23 grants totaling $331,750 were awarded; range of $1,000 - $45,000 per award
Application Information: Write for application guidelines; see the important information in the chapter introduction about the need for institutional affiliation.
Deadline: October 30
Contact: Therese M. Thorn, 2nd Vice President, National Bank of Detroit

Scott (Lillian H. and Karl W.) Foundation
P.O. Box 699
Utica, MI 48087-0699
(313) 731-3300

Description: Funding to organizations providing care and education to children; funding to health agencies.
Restrictions: Limited primarily to Michigan
$ Given: In FY88, 91 grants totaling $53,300 were awarded; range of $100 - $2,500 per award
Application Information: Write for application guidelines; see the important information in the chapter introduction about the need for institutional affiliation.
Deadline: N/A
Contact: B.A. Chaplow, President

MINNESOTA

The Donaldson Foundation

Description: (see full listing information under Illinois)

Hasbro Children's Foundation

Description: (see full listing information under Alabama)

FLOW-THROUGH FUNDING

• • • • • • • • • • • • • • • • • • •

The Emma B. Howe Memorial Foundation
500 Foshay Tower
821 Marquette Ave.
Minneapolis, MN 55402
(612) 339-7343

Description: Special project funding to various charitable organizations, including those which provide health services to prevent, diagnose and treat chronic diseases of children, especially heart and circulatory diseases and cancer.
Restrictions: Limited primarily to Minnesota
$ Given: In FY89, grants totaling $1.3 million were awarded; average range of $10,000 - $50,000 per award
Application Information: Write for application guidelines; see the important information in the chapter introduction about the need for institutional affiliation.
Deadlines: January 15, July 15
Contact: Patricia A. Cummings, Manager - Support Organizations

Keebler Company Foundation

Description: (see full listing information under Colorado)

The Casey Albert T. O'Neil Foundation
c/o First Trust, N.A.
P.O. Box 64704
St. Paul, MN 55164-0704
(612) 291-6240
APPLICATION ADDRESS:
c/o First Trust, N.A.
First National Bank Building
St. Paul, MN 55101

Description: Funding to health agencies and aid to handicapped children, as well as support to Catholic organizations.
Restrictions: Limited primarily to St. Paul, Minnesota
$ Given: In FY89, 99 grants totaling $617,750 were awarded; range of $500 - $35,000 per award; average range of $2,000 - $20,000 per award
Application Information: Write for application guidelines; see the important information in the chapter introduction about the need for institutional affiliation.
Deadline: None
Contact: Sally A. Mullen

US WEST Foundation

Description: (see full listing information under Arizona)

MISSISSIPPI

Hasbro Children's Foundation

Description: (see full listing information under Alabama)

Levi Strauss Foundation

Description: (see full listing information under Arkansas)

MISSOURI

The Donaldson Foundation

Description: (see full listing information under Illinois)

The Green (Allen P. and Josephine B.) Foundation
P.O. Box 523
Mexico, MO 65265
(314) 581-5568

Description: General support for children's health care programs, as well as for many other organizations and concerns.
Restrictions: Focus of giving in the Mexico, Missouri area
$ Given: In 1988, 47 grants totaling $500,600 were awarded; range of $1,000 - $30,000 per award
Application Information: Write for application guidelines; see the important information in the chapter introduction about the need for institutional affiliation.
Deadlines: April 1, October 1
Contact: Walter G. Staley, Secretary-Treasurer

Group Health Plan Foundation of Greater St. Louis
3556 Caroline St.
St. Louis, MO 63104
(314) 577-8105

Description: Funding to health agencies and health service providers is primarily staff- and equipment-related, but special project monies may be applicable to patient needs.
Restrictions: Limited primarily to St. Louis, Missouri
$ Given: In FY88, 8 grants totaling $204,975 were awarded; range of $15,000 - $55,000 per award
Application Information: Write for application guidelines; see the important information in the chapter introduction about the need for institutional affiliation.
Deadline: None
Contact: Robert M. Swanson, Secretary

Hasbro Children's Foundation

Description: (see full listing information under Alabama)

May H. Ilgenfritz Testamentary Trust
108 West Pacific
Sedalia, MO 65301
(816) 826-3310

Description: Funding to a rehabilitation center for handicapped children; additional funding for other concerns.
Restrictions: Funding focused primarily in Missouri
$ Given: In 1988, 1 grant for $35,000 was awarded
Application Information: Write for application guidelines; see the important information in the chapter introduction about the need for institutional affiliation.
Deadline: None
Contact: John Pelham, Trustee

FLOW-THROUGH FUNDING

• • • • • • • • • • • • • • • • • • •

Ewing Marion Kauffman Foundation
922 Walnut St.
Suite 1100
Kansas City, MO 64106
(816) 966-4000
APPLICATION ADDRESS:
9300 Ward Parkway
P.O. Box 8480
Kansas City, MO 64114

Description: Funding focused on health agencies, with additional giving for other concerns.
Restrictions: Limited to Kansas and Missouri. Most funds are disbursed through programs directly administered by the foundation itself; few outright grants are awarded.
$ Given: In FY89, 20 grants totaling $201,639 were awarded; range of $50 - $75,000 per award; plus $478,000 in support for foundation-administered programs
Application Information: Write for application guidelines; see the important information in the chapter introduction about the need for institutional affiliation.
Deadline: None
Contact: Carl Mitchell, Treasurer

Monsanto Fund

Description: (see full listing information under Alabama)

Speas (John W. and Effie E.) Memorial Trust
c/o Boatmen's First
National Bank of
Kansas City
14 West Tenth St.
Kansas City, MO 64183
(816) 691-7481
APPLICATION ADDRESS:
Boatmen's First
National Bank of
Kansas City
P.O. Box 419038
Kansas City, MO 64183

Description: General and special project funding to hospitals and health services, including support for the mentally disabled.
Restrictions: Limited to the greater metropolitan Kansas City area
$ Given: In 1989, 28 grants totaling $1.19 million were awarded; range of $5,000 - $152,000 per award; average range of $5,000 - $100,000 per award
Application Information: Write for application guidelines; see the important information in the chapter introduction about the need for institutional affiliation.
Deadline: None
Contact: David P. Ross, Senior Vice President, Boatmen's First National Bank of Kansas City

Victor E. Speas Foundation
c/o Boatmen's First
National Bank of
Kansas City
14 West Tenth St.
Kansas City, MO 64183
(816) 691-7481

Description: Funding designed specifically to improve the quality of local health care by supporting health care agencies for youth, the handicapped, and others, as well as by supporting medical education and research.
Restrictions: Limited to Jackson, Clay, Platte, and Cass counties of Missouri
$ Given: In 1989, 38 grants totaling $1.26 million were awarded; range of $1,500 - $172,000 per award; average range of $5,000 - $50,000 per award
Application Information: Write for application guidelines; see the important information in the chapter introduction about the need for institutional affiliation.
Deadline: None
Contact: David P. Ross, Senior Vice President, Boatmen's First National Bank of Kansas City

C.W. Titus Foundation
1801 Philtower Building
Tulsa, OK 74103
(918) 582-8095

Description: Funding for hospitals and health services, as well as for the handicapped, and for cultural and social service agencies.
Restrictions: Funding focused primarily in Oklahoma and Missouri
$ Given: In 1988, 43 grants totaling $250,270 were awarded; range of $1,000 - $50,000 per award; average range of $1,000 - $10,000 per award
Application Information: Write for application guidelines; see the important information in the chapter introduction about the need for institutional affiliation.
Deadline: None
Contact: Rosemary T. Reynolds, Trustee

MONTANA

Hasbro Children's Foundation

Description: (see full listing information under Alabama)

Meyer Memorial Trust

Description: (see full listing information under Alaska)

FLOW-THROUGH FUNDING

• • • • • • • • • • • • • • • • • • • •

MPCo/Entech Foundation, Inc.
c/o The M-P-Co.
40 East BRd.way
Butte, MT 59701
(406) 723-5421

Description: Funding for hospitals, health associations, and other organizations.
Restrictions: Funding focused in areas of company operations
$ Given: In 1988, 34 grants totaling $310,159 were awarded; range of $50 - $76,000 per award
Application Information: Write for application guidelines; see the important information in the chapter introduction about the need for institutional affiliation.
Deadline: None
Contact: John Carl, Vice President

US WEST Foundation

Description: (see full listing information under Arizona)

NEBRASKA

Thomas D. Buckley Trust

Description: (see full listing information under Colorado)

Hasbro Children's Foundation

Description: (see full listing information under Alabama)

US WEST Foundation

Description: (see full listing information under Arizona)

Woods Charitable Fund, Inc.
P.O. Box 81309
Lincoln, NE 68501
(402) 474-0707

Description: Funding interests include health clinics, including Sniffles, a children's clinic for the mildly ill, and Healy Mothers and Babies Coalition, both in Chicago, Illinois.
Restrictions: Limited to Chicago, Illinois, and Lincoln, Nebraska areas
$ Given: In 1989, 185 grants totaling $2,285,807; average range, $10,000 - $20,000
Application Information: Write for application guidelines; see the important information in the chapter introduction about the need for institutional affiliation.
Deadlines: January 15, April 15, July 15, and October 15
Contact: Pam Baker

FLOW-THROUGH FUNDING

• • • • • • • • • • • • • • • • • • •

NEVADA

**Hasbro Children's
Foundation**

Description: (see full listing information under Alabama)

**Levi Strauss
Foundation**

Description: (see full listing information under Arkansas)

**Pacific Telesis
Foundation**
Pacific Telesis Center
130 Kearney St.
Room 3351
San Francisco, CA
94108
(415) 394-3693

Description: Funding for a variety of civic and community organizations and programs, including a testing, evaluation and treatment program for children's hearing
Restrictions: Limited to California, Nevada, and other states where Pacific Telesis Group has interests
$ Given: In 1989, 350 grants totaling $8,022,250; range, $500 - $250,000; average range, $2,000 - $50,000
Application Information: Write for application guidelines; see the important information in the chapter introduction about the need for institutional affiliation.
Deadline: None
Contact: Thomas S. Donahoe, President

NEW HAMPSHIRE

**Donaldson (Oliver S.
and Jennie R.)
Charitable Trust**
c/o Durfee Attleboro
Bank
Trust Department
Ten North Main St.
Fall River, MA 02720
(617) 679-8311

Description: Funding for such concerns as hospitals and health care agencies, child welfare and youth agencies, and cancer research and treatment programs.
Restrictions: Giving focused in the Northeast, with emphasis on Massachusetts; preference shown to 11 specific favored institutions
$ Given: In 1987, 37 grants totaling $858,440 were awarded; range of $1,680 - $68,000 per award
Application Information: Write for application guidelines; see the important information in the chapter introduction about the need for institutional affiliation.
Deadline: None; board meets quarterly to consider applications
Contact: William E. Murray, Chair of the Board of Trustees

FLOW-THROUGH FUNDING

• •

Alexander Eastman Foundation
c/o New Hampshire Charitable Fund
One South St.
P.O. Box 1335
Concord, NH 03302-1335
(603) 225-6641

Description: Operating grants and other forms of assistance designed to improve the quality of local health care.
Restrictions: Funding focused in Derry, Londonderry, Windham, Chester, Hampstead, and Sandown, New Hampshire
$ Given: In FY89, 13 grants totaling $125,800 were awarded; range of $2,400 - $30,000 per award; average range of $2,000 - $10,000 per award
Application Information: Write for application guidelines; see the important information in the chapter introduction about the need for institutional affiliation.
Deadlines: February 1, May 1, August 1 and November 1
Contact: Deborah Cowan, Program Director

Foundation for Seacoast Health
P.O. Box 4606
Portsmouth, NH 03801
(603) 433-4001

Description: Support for health care in five areas, two of which are "infants/children" and "adolescents."
Restrictions: Limited to Portsmouth, Rye, New Castle, Greenland, Newington, and North Hampton, New Hampshire; and to Kittery, Eliot and York, Maine
$ Given: In 1989, 39 grants totaling $634,800 were awarded; range of $500 - $125,000 per award
Application Information: Write for application guidelines; see the important information in the chapter introduction about the need for institutional affiliation.
Deadlines: March 1 for infants/children; June 1 for adolescents
Contact: Rodney G. Brock, President

Hasbro Children's Foundation

Description: (see full listing information under Alabama)

Agnes M. Lindsay Trust

Description: (see full listing information under Maine)

J.M. McDonald Foundation, Inc.

Description: (see full listing information under Connecticut)

NEW JERSEY

E.J. Grassman Trust

Description: (see full listing information under Florida)

Hagedorn Fund

Description: (see full listing information under Connecticut)

**Hasbro Children's
Foundation**

Description: (see full listing information under Alabama)

The Hoyt Foundation
Half Acre Rd.
Cranbury, NJ 08512
(609) 655-6000

Description: Although primary focus of support is on education, the foundation also funds hospitals and health agencies.
Restrictions: Funding focused in New Jersey and New York
$ Given: In FY89, 13 grants totaling $147,000 were awarded; range of $1,000 - $38,000 per award
Application Information: Write for application guidelines; see the important information in the chapter introduction about the need for institutional affiliation.
Deadline: None
Contact: Charles O. Hoyt, President

**Innovating Worthy
Projects Foundation**
426 Shore Rd.
Suite E
Somers Point, NJ 08244
(609) 926-1111

Description: Special project funding for preschool medical programs and aid to the handicapped.
Restrictions: N/A
$ Given: In FY89, 25 grants totaling $177,200 were awarded; range of $100 - $75,000 per award
Application Information: Write for application guidelines; see the important information in the chapter introduction about the need for institutional affiliation.
Deadline: None
Contact: Dr. Irving W. Packer, Chair

**Janet Memorial
Foundation**
24-52 Rahway Ave.
Elizabeth, NJ 07202
(201) 527-9393

Description: Funding for child/youth welfare programs, including health service associations.
Restrictions: Limited primarily to Union County, New Jersey
$ Given: In 1988, 20 grants totaling $100,000 were awarded; range of $200 - $10,500 per award
Application Information: Write for application guidelines; see the important information in the chapter introduction about the need for institutional affiliation.
Deadline: September 15
Contact: Alvin W. Taylor, Executive Director

. . . .

Jaqua Foundation
One Garrett Mountain
Plaza
West Paterson, NJ
07424
(201) 278-9790

Description: Direct grants for hospitals and health services, as well as for educational institutions.
Restrictions: N/A
$ Given: In 1988, 23 grants totaling $264,900 were awarded; range of $2,500 - $35,000 per award
Application Information: Write for application guidelines; see the important information in the chapter introduction about the need for institutional affiliation.
Deadline: None
Contact: Eli Hoffman, Chair

J.M. McDonald Foundation, Inc.

Description: (see full listing information under Connecticut)

Monsanto Fund

Description: (see full listing information under Alabama)

George A. Ohl, Jr., Trust
c/o First Fidelity Bank,
N.A., New Jersey
765 BRd. St.
Newark, NJ 07102
(201) 430-4237

Description: Funding with particular focus on health service agencies; additional funding for other projects and organizations.
Restrictions: Limited to New Jersey
$ Given: In 1989, 38 grants totaling $278,750 were awarded; range of $500 - $93,600 per award
Application Information: Write for application guidelines; see the important information in the chapter introduction about the need for institutional affiliation.
Deadlines: February 15, August 15
Contact: James S. Hohn, Vice President, First Fidelity Bank, N.A., New Jersey

Petrie Foundation
70 Enterprise Ave.
Secaucus, NJ 07094-2567

Description: Although giving focuses primarily on cultural institutions, the foundation also supports hospitals and health services, including physical rehabilitation programs.
Restrictions: N/A
$ Given: In 1987, 67 grants totaling $758,170 were awarded; range of $100 - $108,500 per award
Application Information: Write for application guidelines; see the important information in the chapter introduction about the need for institutional affiliation.
Deadline: N/A
Contact: Joseph Flom, Vice President

Union Camp Charitable Trust
c/o Union Camp
Corporation
1600 Valley Rd.
Wayne, NJ 07470
(201) 628-2248

Description: General funding for a wide variety of purposes, including support to hospitals and health services.
Restrictions: Funding focused in areas of corporate operations; support also to some national organizations
$ Given: In 1988, grants totaling $1.73 million were awarded; average range of $200 - $5,000 per award
Application Information: Write for application guidelines; see the important information in the chapter introduction about the need for institutional affiliation.
Deadline: Application submissions preferred January through August
Contact: Sydney N. Phin, Director, Human Resources

The Van Houten (Edward W. and Stella C.) Charitable Trust
c/o First Fidelity Bank,
N.A., New Jersey
765 BRd. St.
Newark, NJ 07102
(201) 430-4533

Description: Funding for various human services, with a special interest in pediatric services at hospitals and health care agencies. Orphaned children and the disabled also receive preference in funding.
Restrictions: Funding focused in Bergen and Passaic counties, New Jersey
$ Given: In FY89, grants totaling $1 million were awarded; average range of $10,000 - $100,0000 per award
Application Information: Write for application guidelines; see the important information in the chapter introduction about the need for institutional affiliation.
Deadlines: February 15, May 15, August 15 and November 15
Contact: James S. Hohn, Vice President, First Fidelity Bank, N.A., New Jersey

Van Pelt Foundation
P.O. Box 823
Westwood, NJ 07675

Description: General purpose funding for small organizations (especially hospitals, AIDS programs, and child welfare agencies) hurt by cutbacks in federal monies or other contributions.
Restrictions: N/A
$ Given: In FY89, 42 grants totaling $278,300 were awarded; range of $200 - $50,000 per award
Application Information: Write for application guidelines; see the important information in the chapter introduction about the need for institutional affiliation.
Deadlines: June 1, December 1
Contact: Lawrence D. Bass, President

NEW MEXICO

FHP Foundation

Description: (see full listing information under Arizona)

FLOW-THROUGH FUNDING

• •

Hasbro Children's Foundation

Description: (see full listing information under Alabama)

Walter Hightower Foundation
c/o Texas Commerce Bank - El Paso
P.O. Drawer 140
El Paso, TX 79980
(915) 546-6515

Description: General purpose funding for the health care of crippled children under age 21. Direct and indirect funding provided.
Restrictions: Limited to western Texas and southern New Mexico
$ Given: In 1988, 1 grant for $250,000 was awarded; an additional 159 grants totaling $25,160 were awarded to individuals; range of $14 - $3,600 per award
Application Information: Write for application guidelines; see the important information in the chapter introduction about the need for institutional affiliation.
Deadline: July 1
Contact: Terry Crenshaw, Charitable Services Officer, Texas Commerce Bank - El Paso

Levi Strauss Foundation

Description: (see full listing information under Arkansas)

US WEST Foundation

Description: (see full listing information under Arizona)

NEW YORK

Albany's Hospital for Incurables
P.O. Box 3628
Executive Park
Albany, NY 12203
(518) 459-7711

Description: General purpose funding designed to support hospitals, hospices, community health centers, regional health planning groups, medical colleges, and nursing homes.
Restrictions: Limited to Albany, Schenectady, Rensselaer, and Saratoga counties of New York
$ Given: In 1989, 17 grants totaling $249,000 were awarded; range of $3,000 - $30,000 per award; average award $15,000
Application Information: Write for application guidelines; see the important information in the chapter introduction about the need for institutional affiliation.
Deadlines: One month before board meetings (board meets in January, April, June, and September)
Contact: Arnold Cogswell, President

• • • • • • • • • • • • • • • • • • •

American Chai Trust
c/o Bernard Perlman
470 Park Ave., South
12th Floor
New York, NY 10016
(212) 889-0575

Description: General purpose funding for health, AIDS, mental health, cancer care, child welfare, and aid to the handicapped, as well as funding for various other human welfare concerns.
Restrictions: N/A
$ Given: In FY89, grants totaling $49,000 were awarded; range of $50 - $2,000 per award; average range of $300 - $2,000 per award
Application Information: Write for application guidelines; see the important information in the chapter introduction about the need for institutional affiliation.
Deadline: None
Contact: Bernard Perlman, Trustee

The Barker Welfare Foundation

Description: (see full listing information under Illinois)

The Albert C. Bostwick Foundation
Hillside Ave. & Bacon Rd.
P.O. Box A
Old Westbury, NY 11568
(516) 334-5566

Description: General funding to hospitals, health service agencies, and aid to the handicapped, as well as to youth services and medical research.
Restrictions: Limited primarily to New York
$ Given: In 1988, 46 grants totaling $114,450 were awarded; range of $150 - $25,000 per award
Application Information: Write for application guidelines; see the important information in the chapter introduction about the need for institutional affiliation.
Deadline: None
Contact: Eleanor P. Bostwick, Trustee

Children's Foundation of Erie County, Inc.
c/o Lewis F. Hazel
292 Northwood Drive
Buffalo, NY 14223
APPLICATION ADDRESS: 55 Rankin Rd., Snyder, NY 14226
(716) 839-1095

Description: Funding for health services, clothing, day care, and camperships for children in financial need; aid to disabled children.
Restrictions: Limited to Erie County, New York
$ Given: In 1988, 34 grants totaling $108,000 were awarded; range of $650 - $7,500 per award
Application Information: Write for application guidelines; see the important information in the chapter introduction about the need for institutional affiliation.
Deadline: January 15
Contact: Mrs. Mary Howland, Grants Chair

The Coca-Cola Foundation, Inc.

Description: (see full listing information under California)

FLOW-THROUGH FUNDING

• • • • • • • • • • • • • • • • • • •

James H. Cummings Foundation, Inc.
1807 Elmwood Ave.
Room 112
Buffalo, NY 14207
(716) 874-0040

Description: Funding for research and charitable provision of health care services to children and elderly populations in specified geographic areas.
Restrictions: Limited to Buffalo, New York; Hendersonville, North Carolina; and Toronto, Ontario
$ Given: In FY89, 25 grants totaling $608,750 were awarded; range of $280 - $100,000 per award
Application Information: Write for application guidelines; see the important information in the chapter introduction about the need for institutional affiliation.
Deadlines: February 1, May 1, August 1, and November 1
Contact: Robert J. Lyle, Executive Director

The Favrot Fund

Description: (see full listing information under California)

Gimbel (Bernard F. and Alva B.) Foundation, Inc.
c/o Carol G. Lebworth
784 Park Ave.
New York, NY 10021
(212) 879-4119

Description: Funding for hospitals, hospices, rehabilitation programs, child welfare agencies, organizations for the disadvantaged, and other concerns.
Restrictions: Funding focused primarily in New York and Connecticut
$ Given: In 1988, 13 grants totaling $109,500 were awarded; range of $1,000 - $25,000 per award
Application Information: Write for application guidelines; see the important information in the chapter introduction about the need for institutional affiliation.
Deadline: None
Contact: Carol G. Lebworth, Co-President

Josephine Goodyear Foundation
1920 Liberty Building
Buffalo, NY 14202
(716) 856-2112

Description: Funding designed to provide for the physical needs of financially distressed women and children; emphasis on hospitals and other local organizations.
Restrictions: Limited to Buffalo, New York
$ Given: In 1988, 34 grants totaling $156,200 were awarded; range of $500 - $25,000 per award
Application Information: Write for application guidelines; see the important information in the chapter introduction about the need for institutional affiliation.
Deadlines: February 1, May 1, September 1 and December 1
Contact: E.W. Dann Stevens, Secretary

Guttman (Stella and Charles) Foundation, Inc.
595 Madison Ave.
Suite 1604
New York, NY 10022
(212) 371-7082

Description: General purpose funding for local organizations providing medical, mental health and physical services, as well as to those providing educational, social and cultural services.
Restrictions: Funding focused primarily in the New York City metropolitan area
$ Given: In 1988, 109 grants totaling $1.11 million were awarded; range of $500 - $300,000 per award; average range of $1,000 - $10,000 per award
Application Information: Write for application guidelines; see the important information in the chapter introduction about the need for institutional affiliation.
Deadline: None
Contact: Elizabeth Olofson, Executive Director

Hagedorn Fund

Description: (see full listing information under Connecticut)

Hasbro Children's Foundation

Description: (see full listing information under Alabama)

The Heckscher Foundation for Children
17 East 47th St.
New York, NY 10017
(212) 371-7775

Description: Funding for child welfare, including support for hospitals, health care, and aid to the handicapped
Restrictions: Funding focused primarily in the greater New York City area
$ Given: In 1988, 116 grants totaling $1.45 million were awarded; range of $1,000 - $100,000 per award; average range of $100 - $25,000 per award
Application Information: Write for application guidelines; see the important information in the chapter introduction about the need for institutional affiliation.
Deadline: None
Contact: Virginia Sloane, President

The Howard and Bush Foundation, Inc.
85 Gillett St.
Hartford, CT 06105
(203) 236-8595

Description: Funding emphasis includes health services
Restrictions: Limited to Hartford, Connecticut and Troy, New York
$ Given: In 1989, 77 grants totaling $1,346,985; range, $3,500 - $72,052; average range, $5,000 - $25,000
Application Information: Write for application guidelines; see the important information in the chapter introduction about the need for institutional affiliation.
Deadlines: February 1, June 1, October 1
Contact: Nancy Roberts

FLOW-THROUGH FUNDING

• •

The Hoyt Foundation
Half Acre Rd.
Cranbury, NJ 08512
(609) 655-6000

Description: Although its primary focus of support is on education, the foundation also funds hospitals and health agencies.
Restrictions: Funding focused in New Jersey and New York
$ Given: In FY89, 13 grants totaling $147,000 were awarded; range of $1,000 - $38,000 per award
Application Information: Write for application guidelines; see the important information in the chapter introduction about the need for institutional affiliation.
Deadline: None
Contact: Charles O. Hoyt, President

**Sid Jacobson
Foundation, Inc.**
151 Sunnyside Blvd.
Plainview, NY 11803-
1589

Description: Funding for Jewish concerns, as well as for hospitals and health services.
Restrictions: N/A
$ Given: In FY89, 88 grants totaling $225,900 were awarded; range of $10 - $125,000 per award
Application Information: Write for application guidelines; see the important information in the chapter introduction about the need for institutional affiliation.
Deadline: None
Contact: Sid Jacobson, Trustee

**Key Food Stores
Foundation, Inc.**
8925 Ave. D
Brooklyn, NY 11236-
1679
(718) 451-1000

Description: Support for Jewish organizations, hospitals and health clinics
Restrictions: N/A
$ Given: In FY89, 29 grants totaling $110,585 were awarded; range of $25 - $69,000 per award
Application Information: Write for application guidelines; see the important information in the chapter introduction about the need for institutional affiliation.
Deadline: None
Contact: Allen Newman, Trustee

• •

The Klau (David and Sadie) Foundation
c/o Rochlin, Lipsky, Goodkin, Stoler & Company, P.C.
510 Fifth Ave.
New York, NY 10036
(212) 840-6444
APPLICATION ADDRESS:
993 Fifth Ave., New York, NY 10028

Description: General funding with focus on hospitals and health care, AIDS programs, and other human and cultural services.
Restrictions: Funding focused in New York City
$ Given: In 1987, 164 grants totaling $649,250 were awarded; range of $10 - $200,000 per award
Application Information: Write for application guidelines; see the important information in the chapter introduction about the need for institutional affiliation.
Deadline: None
Contact: Sadie K. Klau, President

Klock Company Trust
c/o Key Trust Company
253 Wall St.
Kingston, NY 12401
(914) 339-6750

Description: Funding for local hospitals, health services, and other organizations and programs.
Restrictions: Limited to Kingston and Ulster counties of New York
$ Given: In 1988, 28 grants totaling $221,965 were awarded; range of $1,000 - $25,000 per award
Application Information: Write for application guidelines; see the important information in the chapter introduction about the need for institutional affiliation.
Deadlines: Quarterly, in March, June, September, and December
Contact: Earle H. Foster

Frederick McDonald Trust
c/o Norstar Trust Company
69 State St.
Albany, NY 12201
(518) 447-4189

Description: Funding for hospitals and health service agencies
Restrictions: Limited to Albany, New York
$ Given: In 1988, 33 grants totaling $129,500 were awarded; range of $1,000 - $20,000 per award; average range of $2,000 - $4,000 per award
Application Information: Write for application guidelines; see the important information in the chapter introduction about the need for institutional affiliation.
Deadline: October 1
Contact: R.F. Galvin, Senior Trust Officer

J.M. McDonald Foundation, Inc.

Description: (see full listing information under Connecticut)

FLOW-THROUGH FUNDING

• • • • • • • • • • • • • • • • • •

Metzger-Price Fund, Inc.
230 Park Ave.
New York, NY 10169
(212) 867-9500

Description: Funding designed to assist the handicapped and health service agencies
Restrictions: Limited primarily to New York City
$ Given: In FY89, 114 grants totaling $201,000 were awarded; range of $500 - $5,000 per award; average range of $1,000 - $2,500 per award
Application Information: Write for application guidelines; see the important information in the chapter introduction about the need for institutional affiliation.
Deadlines: One month prior to board meetings (board meets in January, April, July, and October)
Contact: Marie Mallot, Secretary-Treasurer

New York Foundation
350 Fifth Ave.
No. 2901
New York, NY 10118
(212) 549-8009

Description: Funding for projects serving the handicapped, the disadvantaged and minorities, especially those projects with a focus on youth or the elderly. Health services, including AIDS programs, are funded. Preference shown to projects with strong community base.
Restrictions: Limited primarily to the New York City area
$ Given: In 1989, 88 grants totaling $2.3 million were awarded; range of $10,000 - $50,000 per award; average range of $20,000 - $35,000 per award
Application Information: Write for application guidelines; see the important information in the chapter introduction about the need for institutional affiliation.
Deadlines: November 1, March 1 and July 1
Contact: Madeline Lee, Executive Director

The Park Foundation

Description: (see full listing information under District of Columbia)

The Spingold (Nate B. and Frances) Foundation, Inc.
c/o Lankenau & Bickford
1740 BRd.way
New York, NY 10019

Description: Funding designed to improve the health care of pediatric and geriatric populations. Although funding seems to be generally staff- and facility-related, special project funding may be applicable to direct patient needs.
Restrictions: Funding focused in New York City and Israel
$ Given: In FY89, 6 grants totaling $222,400 were awarded; range of $12,400 - $75,000 per award; average range of $10,000 - $50,000 per award
Application Information: Write for application guidelines; see the important information in the chapter introduction about the need for institutional affiliation.
Deadline: None
Contact: Daniel L. Kurtz, President

• • • • • • • • • • • • • • • • • • • •

St. Faith's House Foundation
16 Crest Drive
Tarrytown, NY 10591
(914) 631-6065
ADDITIONAL ADDRESS:
P.O. Box 7189
Ardsley-on-Hudson, NY
10503

Description: Grants for services provided to children
Restrictions: Limited to Westchester County, New York
$ Given: In FY89, 24 grants totaling $190,000 were awarded; range of $1,500 - $20,000 per award; average range of $5,000 - $10,000 per award
Application Information: Write for application guidelines; see the important information in the chapter introduction about the need for institutional affiliation.
Deadlines: September 1, December 1 and March 1
Contact: Ann D. Phillips, Chair, Grants Committee

Amy Plant Statter Foundation
598 Madison Ave.
9th Floor
New York, NY 10022

Description: Funding for hospitals, health service agencies, and social services.
Restrictions: N/A
$ Given: In 1987, 43 grants totaling $138,000 were awarded; range of $1,000 - $5,000 per award
Application Information: Write for application guidelines; see the important information in the chapter introduction about the need for institutional affiliation.
Deadline: None
Contact: John H. Reilly, Jr., Trustee

Lawrence A. Wien Foundation, Inc.
c/o Wien, Malkin &
Bettex
60 East 42nd St.
New York, NY 10165

Description: Limited funding for hospitals and health service agencies; giving focus on other human and cultural concerns.
Restrictions: Limited primarily to New York City
$ Given: In FY87, 275 grants totaling $1.5 million were awarded
Application Information: Write for application guidelines; see the important information in the chapter introduction about the need for institutional affiliation.
Deadline: N/A
Contact: Lawrence A. Wien, President

FLOW-THROUGH FUNDING

• •

NORTH CAROLINA

Camp Foundation
P.O. Box 813
Franklin, VA 23851
(804) 562-3439

Description: General and special purpose funding designed to help meet the needs of the local community, including support for hospitals, clinics, and several other local organizations.
Restrictions: Funding focused primarily in the following areas— Franklin, Southampton County, Isle of Wight County, and Tidewater, Virginia; and northeastern North Carolina
$ Given: In 1989, 65 grants totaling $717,250 were awarded; range of $1,000 - $200,000 per award; average range of $1,000 - $20,000 per award
Application Information: Write for application guidelines; see the important information in the chapter introduction about the need for institutional affiliation.
Deadline: September 1; submissions accepted June through August
Contact: Harold S. Atkinson, Executive Director

Community Foundation of Gaston County, Inc.
P.O. Box 123
Gastonia, NC 28053
(704) 864-0927

Description: Medical grants for children age 18 and under; also other forms of financial support to local cultural and youth organizations.
Restrictions: Limited to Gaston County, North Carolina
$ Given: In 1989, grants totaled $484,656
Application Information: Write for application guidelines; see the important information in the chapter introduction about the need for institutional affiliation.
Deadlines: February 15, August 15
Contact: Rebecca B. Carter, Executive Director

James H. Cummings Foundation, Inc.
1807 Elmwood Ave.
Room 112
Buffalo, NY 14207
(716) 874-0040

Description: Funding for research and charitable provision of health care services to children and elderly populations in specified geographical areas.
Restrictions: Limited to Buffalo, New York; Hendersonville, North Carolina; and Toronto, Ontario
$ Given: In FY89, 25 grants totaling $608,750 were awarded; range of $280 - $100,000 per award
Application Information: Write for application guidelines; see the important information in the chapter introduction about the need for institutional affiliation.
Deadlines: February 1, May 1, August 1, and November 1
Contact: Robert J. Lyle, Executive Director

The Duke Endowment
200 North Tryon St.
Suite 1100
Charlotte, NC 28202
(704) 376-0291
ADDITIONAL OFFICE:
3329 Chapel Hill Blvd.
P.O. Box 51307
Durham, NC 27717-1307

Description: Funding to nonprofit hospitals and child care institutions, as well as to several other organizations.
Restrictions: Limited primarily to North Carolina and South Carolina
$ Given: In 1989, 853 grants totaling $45.94 million were awarded
Application Information: Write for application guidelines; see the important information in the chapter introduction about the need for institutional affiliation.
Deadline: None
Contact: Billy G. McCall, Executive Director; or Jere W. Witherspoon, Deputy Executive Director

The Fullerton Foundation, Inc.
515 West Buford St.
Gaffney, SC 29340
(803) 489-6678
APPLICATION ADDRESS:
P.O. Box 1146
Gaffney, SC 29342

Description: Special project and equipment funding for hospitals, health care, and medical research.
Restrictions: Limited primarily to North Carolina and South Carolina
$ Given: In FY88, 34 grants totaling $1.2 million were awarded; range of $1,000 - $132,900 per award
Application Information: Write for application guidelines; see the important information in the chapter introduction about the need for institutional affiliation.
Deadlines: April 1, August 1
Contact: Walter E. Cavell, Executive Director

Hasbro Children's Foundation

Description: (see full listing information under Alabama)

The James M. Johnston Trust for Charitable and Educational Purposes
1101 Vermont Ave., N.W.
Suite 403
Washington, DC 20005
(202) 289-4996

Description: Funding interests include a hospital for sick children
Restrictions: Limited to Washington, DC, and North Carolina
$ Given: In 1988, 85 grants totaling $2,374,150; average range, $10,000 - $30,000
Application Information: Write for application guidelines; see the important information in the chapter introduction about the need for institutional affiliation.
Deadline: None
Contact: Betty Frost Hayes, Chair

Keebler Company Foundation

Description: (see full listing information under Colorado)

FLOW-THROUGH FUNDING

• •

Levi Strauss
Foundation

Description: (see full listing information under Arkansas)

Monsanto Fund

Description: (see full listing information under Alabama)

NORTH DAKOTA

Hasbro Children's
Foundation

Description: (see full listing information under Alabama)

Leach (Tom &
Frances) Foundation,
Inc.
P.O. Box 1136
Bismarck, ND 58502
(701) 255-0479

Description: General funding for hospitals and health service agencies, as well as for other organizations.
Restrictions: Limited primarily to Bismarck and Mandan, North Dakota, and to Tulsa, Oklahoma
$ Given: In 1988, 41 grants totaling $254,500 were awarded; range of $500 - $50,000 per award; average range of $1,000 - $10,000 per award
Application Information: Write for application guidelines; see the important information in the chapter introduction about the need for institutional affiliation.
Deadline: October 1
Contact: Clement C. Weber, Executive Director

US WEST Foundation

Description: (see full listing information under Arizona)

OHIO

Cyclops Foundation
650 Washington Rd.
Pittsburgh, PA 15228
(412) 343-4000

Description: Funding for hospitals, health services, youth and child welfare, and several other concerns.
Restrictions: Funding focused primarily in Pennsylvania and Ohio
$ Given: In 1989, 56 grants totaling $262,636 were awarded; range of $500 - $50,000 per award
Application Information: Write for application guidelines; see the important information in the chapter introduction about the need for institutional affiliation.
Deadline: None
Contact: Susan R. Knapp, Manager - Cash and Banking

Charles H. Dater Foundation, Inc.
508 Atlas Bank Building
Cincinnati, OH 45202
(513) 241-1234

Description: Funding for social services, especially services for children; additional funding for hospitals and educational/cultural concerns.
Restrictions: Funding focused in the Cincinnati, Ohio area
$ Given: In FY89, 31 grants totaling $151,000 were awarded; range of $600 - $20,000 per award
Application Information: Write for application guidelines; see the important information in the chapter introduction about the need for institutional affiliation.
Deadline: None
Contact: Bruce A. Krone, Secretary

Davis Foundation
c/o Huntington National Bank
Trust Department
41 South High St.
Columbus, OH 43260
(614) 463-3707

Description: Funding for a medical center and a college, as well as for aid to crippled children.
Restrictions: Limited primarily to Ohio
$ Given: In 1987, 19 grants totaling $25,400 were awarded; range of $840 - $2,500 per award
Application Information: Write for application guidelines; see the important information in the chapter introduction about the need for institutional affiliation.
Deadline: None
Contact: N/A

Hasbro Children's Foundation

Description: (see full listing information under Alabama)

Iddings Foundation
Kettering Tower
Suite 1620
Dayton, OH 45423
(513) 224-1773

Description: General and special purpose funding for health care, mental health, youth agencies, aid to the handicapped, and various other concerns.
Restrictions: Limited to Ohio, with emphasis on the metropolitan Dayton area
$ Given: In 1988, 67 grants totaling $454,800 were awarded; range of $100 - $30,000 per award; average range of $5 - $10,000 per award
Application Information: Write for application guidelines; see the important information in the chapter introduction about the need for institutional affiliation.
Deadlines: March 1, June 1, September 1 and November 1
Contact: Maribeth A. Eiken, Administrator

FLOW-THROUGH FUNDING

• •

Iowa and Illinois Gas and Electric Company Giving Program

Description: (see full listing information under Illinois)

The Andrew Jergens Foundation
c/o The Central Trust Company, N.A.
P.O. Box 1198
Cincinnati, OH 45201
(513) 651-8377

Description: Special project funding to promote the health and welfare of school-age children.
Restrictions: Limited to the area of Cincinnati, Ohio
$ Given: In FY88, 51 grants totaling $587,000 were awarded; range of $300 - $50,000 per award; average range of $3,000 - $8,000 per award
Application Information: Write for application guidelines; see the important information in the chapter introduction about the need for institutional affiliation.
Deadlines: October 1, January 1, April 1 and July 1
Contact: Nancy C. Gurney, Administrator

Bert William Martin Foundation

Description: (see full listing information under California)

Monsanto Fund

Description: (see full listing information under Alabama)

The Harry C. Moores Foundation
3010 Hayden Rd.
Columbus, OH 43235
(614) 764-8999

Description: Funding for rehabilitation of the handicapped, for hospitals, for agencies serving the retarded, and for various other concerns.
Restrictions: Limited primarily to the Columbus, Ohio area
$ Given: In FY89, 71 grants totaling $879,000 were awarded; range of $1,000 - $200,000 per award; average range of $1,000 - $20,000 per award
Application Information: Write for application guidelines; see the important information in the chapter introduction about the need for institutional affiliation.
Deadline: August 1; submissions accepted October through July
Contact: David L. Fenner, Secretary

The Elisabeth Severance Prentiss Foundation
c/o National City Bank
P.O. Box 5756
Cleveland, OH 44101
(216) 575-2760

Description: General purpose funding to promote public health, including aid to charitable hospitals and health care institutions in Cuyahoga County, Ohio.
Restrictions: Limited to greater Cleveland, Ohio
$ Given: In 1988, 19 grants totaling $2.65 million were awarded; range of $5,000 - $1.23 million per award; average range of $5,000 - $100,000 per award
Application Information: Write for application guidelines; see the important information in the chapter introduction about the need for institutional affiliation.
Deadlines: May 15, November 15
Contact: Frank Dinda

Jacob G. Schmidlapp Trust No. 1
c/o Fifth Third Bank
Department 00864
Foundation Office
Cincinnati, OH 45263
(513) 579-6034

Description: Funding for the relief of sickness, suffering, and distress; for the care of children; and for other related concerns.
Restrictions: Limited primarily to the Cincinnati, Ohio area
$ Given: In FY89, 51 grants totaling $1.55 million were awarded; range of $500 - $250,000 per award; average range of $5,000 - $100,000 per award
Application Information: Write for application guidelines; see the important information in the chapter introduction about the need for institutional affiliation.
Deadlines: February 1, May 1, August 1, and November 1
Contact: Carolyn McCoy

OKLAHOMA

Hasbro Children's Foundation

Description: (see full listing information under Alabama)

Leach (Tom & Frances) Foundation, Inc.
P.O. Box 1136
Bismarck, ND 58502
(701) 255-0479

Description: General funding for hospitals and health service agencies, as well as for other organizations.
Restrictions: Limited primarily to Bismarck and Mandan, North Dakota, and to Tulsa, Oklahoma
$ Given: In 1988, 41 grants totaling $254,500 were awarded; range of $500 - $50,000 per award; average range of $1,000 - $10,000 per award
Application Information: Write for application guidelines; see the important information in the chapter introduction about the need for institutional affiliation.
Deadline: October 1
Contact: Clement C. Weber, Executive Director

FLOW-THROUGH FUNDING

• •

C.W. Titus Foundation
1801 Philtower Building
Tulsa, OK 74103
(918) 582-8095

Description: Funding for hospitals and health services, as well as for the handicapped, and for cultural and social service agencies.
Restrictions: Funding focused primarily in Oklahoma and Missouri
$ Given: In 1988, 43 grants totaling $250,270 were awarded; range of $1,000 - $50,000 per award; average range of $1,000 - $10,000 per award
Application Information: Write for application guidelines; see the important information in the chapter introduction about the need for institutional affiliation.
Deadline: None
Contact: Rosemary T. Reynolds, Trustee

OREGON

The Elizabeth Church Clarke Testamentary Trust/Fund Foundation
c/o Scottish Rite Temple
709 S.W. Fifteenth Ave.
Portland, OR 97205

Description: Funding for medical treatment
Restrictions: Strictly limited to Oregon residents
$ Given: In 1987, grants totaling $52,300 were awarded
Application Information: Write for application guidelines; see the important information in the chapter introduction about the need for institutional affiliation.
Deadline: None
Contact: Walter L. Peters, Executive Secretary, Scottish Rite Temple

Collins Medical Trust
1618 S.W. First Ave.
Suite 300
Portland, OR 97201
(503) 227-1219

Description: Funding for health services and medical research
Restrictions: Limited primarily to Oregon
$ Given: In FY89, 12 grants totaling $147,385 were awarded; range of $1,000 - $25,000 per award
Application Information: Write for application guidelines; see the important information in the chapter introduction about the need for institutional affiliation.
Deadline: None
Contact: Joseph A. Connolly, Administrator

The William G. Gilmore Foundation

Description: (see full listing information under California)

Hasbro Children's Foundation

Description: (see full listing information under Alabama)

Meyer Memorial Trust **Description:** (see full listing information under Alaska)

Public Welfare **Description:** (see full listing information under District of Columbia)
Foundation, Inc.

US WEST Foundation **Description:** (see full listing information under Arizona)

Wheeler Foundation
1211 S.W. Fifth Ave.
Suite 2906
Portland, OR 97204
(503) 228-0261

Description: General purpose funding for medical services and other concerns.
Restrictions: Limited primarily to Oregon
$ Given: In 1988, 63 grants totaling $240,125 were awarded; range of $250 - $20,000 per award; average award $1,000
Application Information: Write for application guidelines; see the important information in the chapter introduction about the need for institutional affiliation.
Deadline: None
Contact: Samuel C. Wheeler, President

PENNSYLVANIA

Ansin Foundation
c/o Charles G. Burke
122 Western Ave.
Lowell, MA 01851

Description: General funding to pre-selected hospitals and health service agencies, as well as to other organizations.
Restrictions: Funding limited primarily to Massachusetts and Pennsylvania
$ Given: In 1988, 15 grants totaling $346,500 were awarded; range of $1,000 - $135,000 per award
Application Information: Recipient hospitals and agencies are pre-selected; ask your case manager or social worker if your hospital has received funding to meet your needs.
Deadline: N/A
Contact: Henry Newell, Manager

FLOW-THROUGH FUNDING

• • • • • • • • • • • • • • • • • • • •

Caroline Alexander
Buck Foundation
1600 Market St.
Suite 3600
Philadelphia, PA 19103

Description: Funding for hospitals and health associations, as well as for various social service programs. Emphasis on children, minorities, and the disabled.
Restrictions: Limited primarily to Pennsylvania, with emphasis on Philadelphia
$ Given: In 1988, 75 grants totaling $113,500 were awarded; range of $1,000 - $6,000 per award
Application Information: Write for application guidelines; see the important information in the chapter introduction about the need for institutional affiliation.
Deadlines: May, November
Contact: J. Pennington Strauss, Trustee

The Clapp (Anne L.
and George H.)
Charitable and
Educational Trust
c/o Mellon Bank, N.A.
One Mellon Bank Center
Pittsburgh, PA 15230
(412) 234-5598

Description: General funding for hospitals, health services, and several other concerns.
Restrictions: Funding focused in Pittsburgh, Pennsylvania
$ Given: In FY88, 37 grants totaling $453,500 were awarded; range of $3,000 - $30,500 per award
Application Information: Write for application guidelines; see the important information in the chapter introduction about the need for institutional affiliation.
Deadline: None
Contact: William B. Outy, Vice President, Mellon Bank, N.A.

Cyclops Foundation
650 Washington Rd.
Pittsburgh, PA 15228
(412) 343-4000

Description: Funding for hospitals, health services, youth and child welfare, and several other concerns.
Restrictions: Funding focused primarily in Pennsylvania and Ohio
$ Given: In 1989, 56 grants totaling $262,636 were awarded; range of $500 - $50,000 per award
Application Information: Write for application guidelines; see the important information in the chapter introduction about the need for institutional affiliation.
Deadline: None
Contact: Susan R. Knapp, Manager - Cash and Banking

Fannie Mae
Foundation

Description: (see full listing information under California)

• •

James T. Hambay Foundation
c/o Dauphin Deposit
Bank & Trust Company
P.O. Box 2961
Harrisburg, PA 17105
(717) 255-2174

Description: Grants for blind, crippled and needy children, to assist with medical and dental expenses. Payments made directly to the attending physician or hospital providing care.
Restrictions: Limited to the area of Harrisburg, Pennsylvania
$ Given: In 1987, 42 grants totaling $104,300 were awarded; range of $50 - $41,300 per award
Application Information: Write for application guidelines; see the important information in the chapter introduction about the need for institutional affiliation.
Deadline: Ongoing; monthly board meetings
Contact: Joseph A. Macri, Trust Officer, Dauphin Deposit Bank & Trust Company

Hasbro Children's Foundation

Description: (see full listing information under Alabama)

Esther Gowen Hood Trust
c/o Mellon Bank (East), N.A.
P.O. Box 7236
Philadelphia, PA 19101
(215) 553-3208

Description: Funding to organizations serving those in need, including health services for youth.
Restrictions: Strictly limited to Philadelphia, Pennsylvania
$ Given: In FY88, 21 grants totaling $57,000 were awarded; range of $1,000 - $5,000 per award
Application Information: Write for application guidelines; see the important information in the chapter introduction about the need for institutional affiliation.
Deadline: April 15
Contact: Pat Kling, Manager

Henry Janssen Foundation, Inc.
2650 Westview Drive
Wyomissing, PA 19610

Description: Funding for hospitals, health care, and other concerns
Restrictions: Funding focused primarily in Pennsylvania, especially in Reading and Berks County
$ Given: In 1988, 41 grants totaling $533,000 were awarded; range of $1,000 - $50,000 per award
Application Information: Write for application guidelines; see the important information in the chapter introduction about the need for institutional affiliation.
Deadline: N/A
Contact: Elsa L. Bowman, President

FLOW-THROUGH FUNDING

• • • • • • • • • • • • • • • • •

Samuel Justus Charitable Trust
P.O. Box 374
Oil City, PA 16301
(814) 677-5085

Description: General purpose funding to assist orphans and delinquent, disadvantaged, and disabled youth.
Restrictions: Limited to Venango County, Pennsylvania
$ Given: In 1986, 25 grants totaling $497,700 were awarded; range of $80 - $49,800 per award; average range of $5,000 - $30,000 per award
Application Information: Write for application guidelines; see the important information in the chapter introduction about the need for institutional affiliation.
Deadlines: April, August, and November submissions preferred
Contact: Stephen P. Kosak, Consultant

Keebler Company Foundation

Description: (see full listing information under Colorado)

Pittsburgh National Bank Foundation
Pittburgh National
Building
14th Floor
Fifth Ave. and Wood St.
Pittsburgh, PA 15222
(412) 762-4222

Description: General purpose funding for hospitals, health care, and other concerns
Restrictions: Limited to southwestern Pennsylvania
$ Given: In 1989, 277 grants totaling $1.54 million were awarded; range of $25 - $363,500 per award; average range of $1,000 - $35,000 per award
Application Information: Write for application guidelines; see the important information in the chapter introduction about the need for institutional affiliation.
Deadline: None
Contact: D. Paul Beard, Secretary

The Harry Plankenhorn Foundation, Inc.
c/o Abram M. Snyder
R.D. 2
Cogan Station, PA
17728

Description: Funding for youth agencies, child welfare, aid to handicapped children, and health and social service agencies.
Restrictions: Limited primarily to Lycoming County, Pennsylvania
$ Given: In 1988, 32 grants totaling $190,000 were awarded; range of $300 - $45,000 per award
Application Information: Write for application guidelines; see the important information in the chapter introduction about the need for institutional affiliation.
Deadline: None
Contact: A. William Gehron, President

• •

Smith Foundation
210 Fairlamb Ave.
Havertown, PA 19083
(215) 446-4651

Description: Funding for the sick and needy; funding for hospitals, child welfare, aid to the handicapped, and other concerns.
Restrictions: Limited to southeastern Pennsylvania
$ Given: In 1988, 67 grants totaling $383,700 were awarded; range of $1,000 - $25,000 per award
Application Information: Write for application guidelines; see the important information in the chapter introduction about the need for institutional affiliation.
Deadline: October 1
Contact: Joseph H. Barber, Secretary-Treasurer

Staunton Farm Foundation Trust
c/o Mellon Bank, N.A.
One Mellon Bank Center
40th Floor
Pittsburgh, PA 15258
APPLICATION ADDRESS:
Philip B. Hallen
3317 Grant Building
Pittsburgh, PA 15219
(412) 261-2485

Description: Funding to local hospitals and agencies focusing on mental health, the emotionally handicapped, and children.
Restrictions: Limited to Allegheny County, Pennsylvania and the surrounding counties
$ Given: In 1987, 18 grants totaling $768,000 were awarded; range of $10,000 - $250,000 per award; average range of $10,000 - $50,000 per award
Application Information: Write for application guidelines; see the important information in the chapter introduction about the need for institutional affiliation.
Deadline: None
Contact: Philip B. Hallen

Widener Memorial Foundation in Aid of Handicapped Children
665 Thomas Rd.
P.O. Box 178
Lafayette Hill, PA 19444
(215) 836-7500

Description: Funding to public and private charitable institutions for the care, education and rehabilitation of orthopedically handicapped children. Research funding for the study of causes, treatment and prevention of such handicaps.
Restrictions: Limited to Delaware Valley, Pennsylvania
$ Given: In 1989, 13 grants totaling $708,800 were awarded; range of $3,200 - $235,000 per award; average range of $15,000 - $100,000 per award
Application Information: Write for application guidelines; see the important information in the chapter introduction about the need for institutional affiliation.
Deadlines: April 15, October 15
Contact: F. Eugene Dixon, Jr., President

FLOW-THROUGH FUNDING

. . . .

RHODE ISLAND

Donaldson (Oliver S. and Jennie R.) Charitable Trust
c/o Durfee Attleboro Bank
Trust Department
Ten North Main St.
Fall River, MA 02720
(617) 679-8311

Description: Funding for such concerns as hospitals and health care agencies, child welfare and youth agencies, and cancer research and treatment programs.
Restrictions: Giving focused in the Northeast, with emphasis on Massachusetts; preference shown to 11 specific favored institutions
$ Given: In 1987, 37 grants totaling $858,440 were awarded; range of $1,680 - $68,000 per award
Application Information: Write for application guidelines; see the important information in the chapter introduction about the need for institutional affiliation.
Deadline: None; board meets quarterly to consider applications
Contact: William E. Murray, Chair of the Board of Trustees

Hasbro Children's Foundation

Description: (see full listing information under Alabama)

J.M. McDonald Foundation, Inc.

Description: (see full listing information under Connecticut)

Prince Charitable Trusts

Description: (see full listing information under Illinois)

SOUTH CAROLINA

The Duke Endowment
200 North Tryon St.
Suite 1100
Charlotte, NC 28202
(704) 376-0291
ADDITIONAL OFFICE:
3329 Chapel Hill Blvd.
P.O. Box 51307
Durham, NC 27717-1307

Description: Funding to nonprofit hospitals and child care institutions, as well as to several other organizations.
Restrictions: Limited primarily to North Carolina and South Carolina
$ Given: In 1989, 853 grants totaling $45.94 million were awarded
Application Information: Write for application guidelines; see the important information in the chapter introduction about the need for institutional affiliation.
Deadline: None
Contact: Billy G. McCall, Executive Director; or Jere W. Witherspoon, Deputy Executive Director

144

The Fullerton Foundation, Inc.
515 West Buford St.
Gaffney, SC 29340
(803) 489-6678
APPLICATION ADDRESS:
P.O. Box 1146
Gaffney, SC 29342

Description: Special project and equipment funding for hospitals, health care, and medical research.
Restrictions: Limited primarily to North Carolina and South Carolina
$ Given: In FY88, 34 grants totaling $1.2 million were awarded; range of $1,000 - $132,900 per award
Application Information: Write for application guidelines; see the important information in the chapter introduction about the need for institutional affiliation.
Deadlines: April 1, August 1
Contact: Walter E. Cavell, Executive Director

Hasbro Children's Foundation

Description: (see full listing information under Alabama)

Monsanto Fund

Description: (see full listing information under Alabama)

SOUTH DAKOTA

Hasbro Children's Foundation

Description: (see full listing information under Alabama)

US WEST Foundation

Description: (see full listing information under Arizona)

TENNESSEE

Camelot Foundation, Inc.
108 West Price Lane
Oak Ridge, TN 37830
(615) 482-1492

Description: Funding designated specifically for the care and treatment of disturbed children.
Restrictions: N/A
$ Given: In FY89, 1 grant for $40,000 was awarded
Application Information: Write for application guidelines; see the important information in the chapter introduction about the need for institutional affiliation.
Deadline: None
Contact: John F. Terrell, Sr., Manager

FLOW-THROUGH FUNDING

• •

Christy-Houston Foundation, Inc.
122 North Spring St.
Murfreesboro, TN 37130
(615) 898-1140

Description: Funding for hospitals and health-related projects
Restrictions: Limited to Rutherford County, Tennessee
$ Given: In FY88, 5 grants totaling $158,245 were awarded; range of $16,000 - $50,000 per award
Application Information: Write for application guidelines; see the important information in the chapter introduction about the need for institutional affiliation.
Deadline: January 31
Contact: James R. Arnhart, Executive Director

Hargis (Estes H. & Florence Parker) Charitable Foundation

Description: (see full listing information under Alabama)

Hasbro Children's Foundation

Description: (see full listing information under Alabama)

Levi Strauss Foundation

Description: (see full listing information under Arkansas)

TEXAS

ARCO Foundation

Description: (see full listing information under Alaska)

The Cain (Effie and Wofford) Foundation
6116 North Central Expressway
Suite 909-LB65
Dallas, TX 75206
(214) 361-4201

Description: Although funding is primarily directed to cultural and educational programs, monies are also available for medical services, aid to the handicapped, and other concerns.
Restrictions: Limited to Texas
$ Given: In FY89, 56 grants totaling $1.6 million were awarded; range of $500 - $500,000 per award; average range of $2,000 - $35,000 per award
Application Information: Write for application guidelines; see the important information in the chapter introduction about the need for institutional affiliation.
Deadline: August 31
Contact: Harvey L. Walker, Executive Director

• • • • • • • • • • • • • • • • • • • •

The Coca-Cola Foundation, Inc.

Description: (see full listing information under California)

Fannie Mae Foundation

Description: (see full listing information under California)

The Favrot Fund

Description: (see full listing information under California)

The Frees Foundation
5373 West Alabama
Suite 404
Houston, TX 77056
(713) 623-0515

Description: Funding for hospitals, health services, and other organizations and concerns serving Texas and the Republic of Mexico.
Restrictions: Limited primarily to Texas and Mexico
$ Given: In 1989, 13 grants totaling $153,600 were awarded; range of $300 - $100,000 per award; average range of $1,000 - $100,000 per award
Application Information: Write for application guidelines; see the important information in the chapter introduction about the need for institutional affiliation.
Deadline: None
Contact: Nancy Frees Rosser, Director

The Green Foundation
3300 First City Center
Dallas, TX 75201
(214) 969-1700

Description: General funding for hospitals and medical services, as well as for other concerns.
Restrictions: Funding focused primarily in Dallas, Texas
$ Given: In 1988, 26 grants totaling $482,150 were awarded; range of $250 - $150,000 per award
Application Information: Write for application guidelines; see the important information in the chapter introduction about the need for institutional affiliation.
Deadline: None
Contact: William E. Collins, Trustee

FLOW-THROUGH FUNDING

• • • • • • • • • • • • • • • • • • •

The Hamman (George and Mary Josephine) Foundation
910 Travis St.
No. 1438
Houston, TX 77002-5816
(713) 658-8345

Description: Funding for hospitals and medical treatment, as well as for numerous other concerns.
Restrictions: Limited to Texas, with emphasis on the Houston area
$ Given: In FY89, grants totaled $637,400; range of $500 - $65,000 per award; average range of $1,000 - $10,000 per award
Application Information: Write for application guidelines; see the important information in the chapter introduction about the need for institutional affiliation.
Deadline: None
Contact: Stephen I. Gelsey, Administrator

Hasbro Children's Foundation

Description: (see full listing information under Alabama)

Walter Hightower Foundation
c/o Texas Commerce Bank - El Paso
P.O. Drawer 140
El Paso, TX 79980
(915) 546-6515

Description: General purpose funding for the health care of crippled children under age 21. Direct and indirect funding provided.
Restrictions: Limited to western Texas and southern New Mexico
$ Given: In 1988, 1 grant for $250,000 was awarded; an additional 159 grants totaling $25,160 were awarded to individuals; range of $14 - $3,600 per award
Application Information: Write for application guidelines; see the important information in the chapter introduction about the need for institutional affiliation.
Deadline: July 1
Contact: Terry Crenshaw, Charitable Services Officer, Texas Commerce Bank - El Paso

Hoblitzelle Foundation
1410 Tower 1
NCNB Center
Dallas, TX 75201
(214) 979-0321

Description: General purpose and special project funding for hospitals and health services, as well as for educational, cultural and social concerns.
Restrictions: Limited to Texas, with emphasis on Dallas
$ Given: In FY89, 59 grants totaling $3.29 million were awarded; range of $200 - $300,000 per award; average award $60,000
Application Information: Write for application guidelines; see the important information in the chapter introduction about the need for institutional affiliation.
Deadlines: April 15, August 15 and December 15
Contact: Paul W. Harris, Executive Vice President

• • • • • • • • • • • • • • • • • • • •

Keebler Company
Foundation

Description: (see full listing information under Colorado)

Levi Strauss
Foundation

Description: (see full listing information under Arkansas)

Monsanto Fund

Description: (see full listing information under Alabama)

The Moody
Foundation
704 Moody National
Bank Building
Galveston, TX 77550
(409) 763-5333

Description: Special purpose funding for the promotion of health and science, as well as for cultural and social concerns.
Restrictions: Limited to Texas
$ Given: In 1988, 79 grants totaling $15.46 million were awarded; range of $10,000 - $150,000 per award
Application Information: Write for application guidelines; see the important information in the chapter introduction about the need for institutional affiliation.
Deadlines: Six weeks prior to quarterly board meetings
Contact: Peter M. Moore, Grants Officer

Dora Roberts
Foundation
c/o Texas American
Bridge Bank/Fort Worth
P.O. Box 2050
Fort Worth, TX 76113
(817) 884-4442

Description: General purpose funding for hospitals, health services, and a specified rehabilitation center, as well as for educational, social service, and religious concerns.
Restrictions: Limited to Texas, with emphasis on Big Spring
$ Given: In 1989, 20 grants totaling $874,294 were awarded; range of $780 - $230,000 per award
Application Information: Write for application guidelines; see the important information in the chapter introduction about the need for institutional affiliation.
Deadline: September 30
Contact: Rick Piersall, Vice President and Trust Officer, Texas American Bridge Bank/Fort Worth

FLOW-THROUGH FUNDING

· · · · · · · · · · · · · · · · · · · ·

**Seymour (W.L. &
Louise E.) Foundation**
c/o MTrust El Paso,
N.A.
P.O. Box 1072
El Paso, TX 79958
(915) 546-4369

Description: Funding for handicapped and homeless children
Restrictions: Limited primarily to El Paso, Texas
$ Given: In FY87, 4 grants totaling $83,000 were awarded; range
of $1,000 - $50,000 per award; average award $20,000
Application Information: Write for application guidelines; see
the important information in the chapter introduction about the
need for institutional affiliation.
Deadline: None
Contact: Dorothy Hart, Vice President and Trust Officer, MTrust
El Paso, N.A.

**H.E. Stumberg, Sr.
Orphans, Crippled
Children &
Handicapped Persons
Trust**
Tower Life Building
Suite 701
San Antonio, TX 78205
(512) 225-0243

Description: General purpose funding to organizations that serve
handicapped and crippled children and adults.
Restrictions: Funding focused primarily in Bexar County, Texas
$ Given: In 1988, 21 grants totaling $49,000 were awarded;
range of $250 - $8,500 per award
Application Information: Write for application guidelines; see
the important information in the chapter introduction about the
need for institutional affiliation.
Deadline: October 31
Contact: Louis H. Stumberg, Trustee

**Turner Charitable
Foundation**
811 Rusk St.
Suite 205
Houston, TX 77002
(713) 237-1117

Description: General and special purpose funding for hospitals
and health services, as well as for a wide variety of educational,
cultural, religious, and social welfare concerns.
Restrictions: Limited to Texas
$ Given: In FY89, 57 grants totaling $426,100 were awarded;
range of $500 - $75,000 per award; average range of $1,000 -
$5,000 per award
Application Information: Write for application guidelines; see
the important information in the chapter introduction about the
need for institutional affiliation.
Deadline: March 15
Contact: Eyvonne Moser, Assistant Secretary

The Vale-Asche Foundation
910 River Oaks Bank Building
2001 Kirby Drive
Suite 910
Houston, TX 77019
(713) 520-7334

Description: Special project funding for health care, child welfare, medical research, aid to the handicapped, and various other concerns.
Restrictions: Funding focused primarily in Houston, Texas
$ Given: In FY88, 19 grants totaling $207,000 were awarded; range of $1,000 - $30,000 per award
Application Information: Write for application guidelines; see the important information in the chapter introduction about the need for institutional affiliation.
Deadline: None; requests reviewed annually in September/October
Contact: Mrs. Vale Asche Ackerman, President

Lola Wright Foundation, Inc.
P.O. Box 1138
Georgetown, TX 78627-1138
(512) 255-3067

Description: Special purpose funding and continuing support for hospitals, health care services, AIDS programs, services for the handicapped, and several other concerns.
Restrictions: Limited to Texas, with emphasis on the Austin area
$ Given: In 1987, grants totaling $564,884 were awarded; range of $1,500 - $25,000 per award
Application Information: Write for application guidelines; see the important information in the chapter introduction about the need for institutional affiliation.
Deadlines: April 1, October 1
Contact: Patrick H. O'Donnell, President

UTAH

The Dumke (Dr. Ezekiel R. and Edna Wattis) Foundation

Description: (see full listing information under Idaho)

Willard L. Eccles Charitable Foundation
P.O. Box 45385
Salt Lake City, UT 84145-0385
(801) 532-1500

Description: Funding for health care, medical research and medical education.
Restrictions: Limited primarily to Utah, with emphasis on the Odgen, Utah area
$ Given: In FY88, 15 grants totaling $1 million were awarded; range of $2,000 - $235,000 per award; average range of $10,000 - $150,000 per award
Application Information: Write for application guidelines; see the important information in the chapter introduction about the need for institutional affiliation.
Deadlines: Month prior to board meetings (March, June and October)
Contact: Clark P. Giles, Secretary

FLOW-THROUGH FUNDING

• • • • • • • • • • • • • • • • • • •

FHP Foundation

Description: (see full listing information under Arizona)

Hasbro Children's Foundation

Description: (see full listing information under Alabama)

Powell (Samuel C. & Myra G.) Foundation
c/o First Security Bank of Utah, N.A.
P.O. Box 9936
Ogden, UT 84409
(801) 393-5376
APPLICATION ADDRESS:
714 Eccles Building
385 24th St.
Ogden, UT 84401

Description: Funding for health care and hospitals, including a surgical society and a burn center; additional funding for a wide variety of other concerns.
Restrictions: Limited primarily to Ogden and Salt Lake City, Utah
$ Given: In 1988, 11 grants totaling $27,775 were awarded; range of $100 - $10,000 per award
Application Information: Write for application guidelines; see the important information in the chapter introduction about the need for institutional affiliation.
Deadline: September 30
Contact: Samuel H. Barker, Chair

Dr. Scholl Foundation
11 South LaSalle St.
Suite 2100
Chicago, IL 60603
(312) 782-5210

Description: Supports programs for children, grants to hospitals, and medical and nursing institutions, including a community nursing service in Salt Lake City, Utah.
Restrictions: No geographic limitations
$ Given: In 1989, 372 grants totaling $7,371,300; range, $1,000 - $200,000; average range, $5,000 - $50,000
Application Information: Write for application guidelines; see the important information in the chapter introduction about the need for institutional affiliation.
Deadline: May 15
Contact: Jack E. Scholl, Executive Director

US WEST Foundation

Description: (see full listing information under Arizona)

• • • • • • • • • • • • • • • • • • • •

VERMONT

**Hasbro Children's
Foundation**

Description: (see full listing information under Alabama)

**Agnes M. Lindsay
Trust**
45 Market St.
Manchester, NH 03101
(603) 669-4140

Description: General funding focused on child welfare and health services, as well as services for the handicapped.
Restrictions: Limited to Maine, Massachusetts, New Hampshire, and Vermont
$ Given: In 1988, 191 grants totaling $863,771 were awarded; range of $1,000 - $10,000 per award
Application Information: Write for application guidelines; see the important information in the chapter introduction about the need for institutional affiliation.
Deadline: Proposals considered monthly
Contact: Robert L. Chiesa, Trustee

**J.M. McDonald
Foundation, Inc.**

Description: (see full listing information under Connecticut)

VIRGINIA

Camp Foundation
P.O. Box 813
Franklin, VA 23851
(804) 562-3439

Description: General and special purpose funding designed to help meet the needs of the local community, including support for hospitals, clinics, and several other local organizations.
Restrictions: Funding focused primarily in the following areas— Franklin, Southampton County, Isle of Wight County, and Tidewater, Virginia; and northeastern North Carolina
$ Given: In 1989, 65 grants totaling $717,250 were awarded; range of $1,000 - $200,000 per award; average range of $1,000 - $20,000 per award
Application Information: Write for application guidelines; see the important information in the chapter introduction about the need for institutional affiliation.
Deadline: September 1; submissions accepted June through August
Contact: Harold S. Atkinson, Executive Director

FLOW-THROUGH FUNDING

. . . .

CSG Foundation, Inc.
8401 Connecticut Ave.
Chevy Chase, MD 20815
(301) 652-6880

Description: Funding to organizations serving children
Restrictions: Funding focused primarily in the Washington, DC area
$ Given: In 1988, 1 grant for $45,000 was awarded
Application Information: Write for application guidelines; see the important information in the chapter introduction about the need for institutional affiliation.
Deadline: None
Contact: W. Shepherdson Abell, Secretary-Treasurer

Jesse Ball duPont Religious, Charitable and Educational Fund
225 Water St.
Suite 1200
Jacksonville, FL 32202-4424
(904) 353-0890

Description: Funding interests include health organizations and hospitals, including a clinic for newborn infants and their mothers in Gainesville, Florida.
Restrictions: Limited primarily to Florida, Delaware, and Virginia; limited to organizations receiving funds from the donor from 1960 to 1964
$ Given: In FY89, 109 grants totaling $5,034,391; average range, $5,000 - $100,000
Application Information: Write for application guidelines; see the important information in the chapter introduction about the need for institutional affiliation.
Deadline: None
Contact: George Penick, Executive Director

Hasbro Children's Foundation

Description: (see full listing information under Alabama)

Levi Strauss Foundation

Description: (see full listing information under Arkansas)

Little River Foundation
Whitewood Farm
The Plains, VA 22171
(703) 253-5540

Description: General support and medical research funding primarily directed to hospitals; funding for AIDS and drug abuse programs; additional funding to address a variety of concerns.
Restrictions: N/A
$ Given: In FY89, 48 grants totaling $289,500 were awarded; range of $500 - $30,000 per award
Application Information: Write for application guidelines; see the important information in the chapter introduction about the need for institutional affiliation.
Deadline: None
Contact: Dale D. Hogoboom, Assistant Treasurer

• • • • • • • • • • • • • • • • • • • •

George Preston
Marshall Foundation

Description: (see full listing information under District of Columbia)

Massey Foundation
P.O. Box 26765
Richmond, VA 23261
(804) 788-1800

Description: Limited funding for hospitals and health services; primary focus on education.
Restrictions: Limited primarily to Virginia, with emphasis on Richmond
$ Given: In FY89, 76 grants totaling $1.37 million were awarded; range of $1,000 - $210,000 per award; average range of $1,000 - $25,000 per award
Application Information: Write for application guidelines; see the important information in the chapter introduction about the need for institutional affiliation.
Deadline: None
Contact: William E. Massey, Jr., President

The Memorial
Foundation for
Children
c/o Capitoline
Investment Services, Inc.
P.O. Box 436
Richmond, VA 23203-
0436
APPLICATION ADDRESS:
P.O. Box 8342
Richmond, VA 23226

Description: Funding for nonprofit groups, designated for the care and education of children.
Restrictions: Limited to the Richmond, Virginia area
$ Given: In 1988, 36 grants totaling $317,000 were awarded; range of $2,000 - $20,250 per award
Application Information: Write for application guidelines; see the important information in the chapter introduction about the need for institutional affiliation.
Deadline: September 1
Contact: Mrs. Jack Spain, Jr., Chair, Grant Committee

Metropolitan Health
Foundation, Inc.
700 West Grace St.
Richmond, VA 23220
(804) 643-1958

Description: General support funding specifically for health-related programs.
Restrictions: Limited primarily to the Richmond, Virginia area
$ Given: In 1988, 11 grants totaling $73,400 were awarded; range of $500 - $3,500 per award
Application Information: Write for application guidelines; see the important information in the chapter introduction about the need for institutional affiliation.
Deadline: None
Contact: Charles P. Winkler, M.D., President

FLOW-THROUGH FUNDING

• • • • • • • • • • • • • • • • • • • •

Meyer (Eugene and Agnes E.) Foundation

Description: (see full listing information under District of Columbia)

Public Welfare Foundation, Inc.
2600 Virginia Ave., N.W.
Room 505
Washington, DC 20037-1977
(202) 965-1800

Description: Funding interests include a pediatric health care clinic in Portland, Oregon and a youth health clinic in Elkins, VA.
Restrictions: No geographic restrictions
$ Given: In FY89, 341 grants totaling $12,331,100; range, $5,000 - $240,000; average, $36,000
Application Information: Write for application guidelines; see the important information in the chapter introduction about the need for institutional affiliation.
Deadline: None
Contact: C. Glenn Ihrig, Executive Director

WASHINGTON

The William G. Gilmore Foundation
120 Montgomery St.
Suite 1880
San Francisco, CA 94104
(415) 546-1400

Description: General purpose funding and emergency funding for health services and AIDS programs, as well as for several other community-based organizations.
Restrictions: Funding focused primarily in California, Oregon and Washington
$ Given: In 1988, 132 grants totaling $766,345 were awarded; range of $200 - $50,000 per award; average range of $500 - $5,000 per award
Application Information: Write for application guidelines; see the important information in the chapter introduction about the need for institutional affiliation.
Deadlines: May 1, November 1
Contact: Faye Wilson, Secretary

Glaser Foundation, Inc.
P.O. Box N
Edmonds, WA 98020

Description: Special purpose funding for health agencies and agencies serving children, youth and the handicapped; additional funding to address drug abuse.
Restrictions: Funding focused primarily in the Puget Sound area of Washington
$ Given: In FY89, 62 grants totaling $236,800 were awarded; range of $50 - $10,250 per award; average range of $1,000 - $5,000 per award
Application Information: Write for application guidelines; see the important information in the chapter introduction about the need for institutional affiliation.
Deadline: None
Contact: R.W. Carlstrom, Executive Director

· ·

Hasbro Children's Foundation

Description: (see full listing information under Alabama)

George Frederick Jewett Foundation
One Maritime Plaza
Suite 990
San Francisco, CA
94111
(415) 421-1351

Description: General and special purpose funding to address a wide variety of human welfare concerns, including funding for health care and medical services.
Restrictions: Funding focused primarily in the Pacific Northwest, especially in northern Idaho, eastern Washington (with emphasis on Spokane), and San Francisco, California
$ Given: In 1989, 134 grants totaling $953,600 were awarded; range of $500 - $25,000 per award; average range of $1,000 - $15,000 per award
Application Information: Write for application guidelines; see the important information in the chapter introduction about the need for institutional affiliation.
Deadlines: February 15, May 15, August 15, and November 1
Contact: Theresa A. Mullen, Program Director

Meyer Memorial Trust

Description: (see full listing information under Alaska)

The Schoenfeld-Gardner Foundation
Columbia Center
47th Floor
Seattle, WA 98104

Description: Funding to hospitals, health agencies, and social service agencies, including youth and child welfare agencies.
Restrictions: Limited primarily to Washington
$ Given: In FY87, 65 grants totaling $72,700 were awarded; range of $200 - $30,000 per award
Application Information: Write for application guidelines; see the important information in the chapter introduction about the need for institutional affiliation.
Deadline: None
Contact: Trustees

US West Foundation

Description: (see full listing information under Arizona)

FLOW-THROUGH FUNDING

• •

WEST VIRGINIA

Hasbro Children's Foundation
32 West 23rd St.
New York, NY 10010
(212) 645-2400

Description: Funding designated for improving children's quality of life; emphasis on health care programs, including pediatric AIDS programs, and on education for the handicapped.
Restrictions: Funding to direct service providers is given on a nationwide basis; limited to programs involving children under the age of 12
$ Given: In 1988, 54 grants totaling $1.7 million were awarded; range of $500 - $150,000 per award; average range of $5,000 - $150,000 per award
Application Information: Write for application guidelines; see the important information in the chapter introduction about the need for institutional affiliation.
Deadlines: Two months prior to board meetings (board meets in February, June, and October)
Contact: Eve Weiss, Executive Director

Monsanto Fund

Description: (see full listing information under Alabama)

WISCONSIN

John Deere Foundation

Description: (see full listing information under Illinois)

Edward U. Demmer Foundation
c/o Bank One Wisconsin
Trust Company, N.A.
P.O. Box 1308
Milwaukee, WI 53201
(414) 765-2800

Description: Funding emphasis on projects related to children, including support for hospitals and health care agencies.
Restrictions: Limited primarily to Wisconsin; Protestant or non-sectarian institutions only
$ Given: In 1988, 36 grants totaling $289,600 were awarded; range of $1,000 - $100,000 per award
Application Information: Write for application guidelines; see the important information in the chapter introduction about the need for institutional affiliation.
Deadline: None
Contact: Robert L. Hanley, Senior Vice President, Bank One Wisconsin Trust Company, N.A.

The Donaldson Foundation

Description: (see full listing information under Illinois)

Ralph Evinrude
Foundation, Inc.

Description: (see full listing information under Florida)

Harnischfeger
Foundation, Inc.
120 Bishops Way
Suite 161
Brookfield, WI 53005
(414) 784-4679

Description: General funding for hospitals and health care, as well as for youth agencies and other organizations.
Restrictions: N/A
$ Given: In 1989, 35 grants totaling $110,000 were awarded; range of $100 - $10,000 per award
Application Information: Write for application guidelines; see the important information in the chapter introduction about the need for institutional affiliation.
Deadline: N/A; board meets in May and November
Contact: Henry Harnischfeger, President

Hasbro Children's
Foundation

Description: (see full listing information under Alabama)

Johnson Controls
Foundation
5757 No. Green Bay Ave.
P.O. Box 591
Milwaukee, WI 53201
(414) 228-2219

Description: Funding for health services and hospitals, for services to the handicapped, for care of children, and for a variety of other civic and cultural concerns.
Restrictions: No funding for political or religious purposes
$ Given: In 1988, 1753 grants totaling $3.01 million were awarded
Application Information: Write for application guidelines; see the important information in the chapter introduction about the need for institutional affiliation.
Deadline: None
Contact: Florence R. Klatt, Member, Advisory Board

The Elmer Leach
Foundation, Inc.
c/o First Wisconsin
National Bank of
Oshkosh
P.O. Box 2448
Oshkosh, WI 54903

Description: Funding to assist children with medical needs; additional funding for educational concerns.
Restrictions: Limited primarily to Oshkosh, Wisconsin
$ Given: In 1987, grants totaling $58,700 were awarded
Application Information: Write for application guidelines; see the important information in the chapter introduction about the need for institutional affiliation.
Deadline: Applications accepted January 1 through November 1
Contact: David C. Leach, President

FLOW-THROUGH FUNDING

• • • • • • • • • • • • • • • • • • • •

**Faye McBeath
Foundation**
1020 North BRd.way
Milwaukee, WI 53202
(414) 272-2626

Description: Funding to improve the welfare of several populations, including funding for the medical, nursing and hospital care of the sick and disabled.
Restrictions: Limited to Wisconsin, with emphasis on Milwaukee
$ Given: In 1989, 53 grants totaling $1.4 million were awarded; range of $15,000 - $75,000 per award; average range of $10,000 - $40,000 per award
Application Information: Write for application guidelines; see the important information in the chapter introduction about the need for institutional affiliation.
Deadline: Ongoing
Contact: Sarah M. Dean, Executive Director

**Sundstrand
Corporation Foundation**

Description: (see full listing information under Illinois)

WYOMING

**Hasbro Children's
Foundation**

Description: (see full listing information under Alabama)

**Tonkin (Tom and
Helen) Foundation**
c/o Wyoming National
Bank Casper
P.O. Box 2799
Casper, WY 82602
(307) 266-1100

Description: General and emergency funding to help local youth, especially those who are ill, injured, or in financial distress.
Restrictions: Limited to Wyoming, with emphasis on Casper; individuals in need must be ages 6-21
$ Given: In FY89, 20 grants totaling $86,000 were awarded; range of $900 - $15,300 per award; average range of $1,000 - $10,000 per award
Application Information: Write for application guidelines; see the important information in the chapter introduction about the need for institutional affiliation.
Deadline: None
Contact: Elona Anderson

US WEST Foundation

Description: (see full listing information under Arizona)

State and Regional Government Grants

This chapter lists state and regional government agencies that can be of assistance in your search for funding. For the most part, these agencies represent a local level of access to federal funding programs and organizations. For example, the Department of Health and Human Services (DHHS) has several regional offices; groups applying for funds from a DHHS national program (such as "Community Health Centers") must make their applications through their regional offices. Because each government agency administers several different funding programs, and because monies available vary from year to year, the state-by-state information provided here is, for the most part, listed in a generic form. For details about the federal funding programs administered through these regional offices, please refer to the next chapter, "Federal Grants."

Also included in this chapter are Native and Indian Health Service grants, which provide funding for American Indians and Native Alaskans. These grants are administered through local offices serving their immediate areas. Money is awarded directly to federally-recognized tribes or tribal organizations which, in turn, use the money to provide health-related services to tribal members who need them.

Individuals cannot apply directly to these sources for funding. The grant programs listed in this chapter require that a nonprofit organization, government agency, or tribal organization be the direct recipient of funds. In order to receive financial support from these state and regional sources, you must work through a sponsor organization. This is a form of flow-through funding; for a detailed discussion of how and why to

. . . .

find a nonprofit sponsor, please see the introduction to the "Flow-Through Funding" chapter.

The price of health care is a major and growing worry for federal, state and local governments, which must devote a rising share of their strained budgets to paying for health care. More than forty percent of the nation's health bills are now covered by government programs. Despite this, federal monies still exist.

Although you cannot make a direct application to any of the sources in this chapter, your background work can be of immense help to your sponsor organization. Use the information provided in this chapter to identify funding programs that seem to address your specific situation. Make a list of what it is you need monies for (i.e., hospital bills, long-term care costs, loss of income replacement). Ask yourself such questions as, are there demonstrated financial needs on the part of the patient or the patient's family? In this fashion, you can be ready to address every issue leading to support and aid in one telephone call — by being able to describe precisely the kinds of funding for which you may be eligible.

Next, call the potential funding sources and ask this: "What types of funding programs do you provide?" If the response does not include a program that meets your particular needs, ask more specific questions. **Make it clear that you have a sponsor arrangement with an appropriate organization.** If the agency you call does not offer a program to meet your needs, someone there may be able to direct you to an agency that does. If the agency publishes materials describing its funding programs, request that these be mailed to you, along with an application. Also make sure to find out if there is a deadline coming up, so that you and your sponsor will be able to return any applications by that time.

. . . .

ALABAMA

Appalachian Regional Commission
State Alternate's Office
Department of Economic and Community Affairs
Box 250347
3465 Norman Bridge Road
Montgomery, AL 36125-0347
(205) 242-8672

Program: Appalachian 202 Health Programs (Federal program 23.004)
Description: Project grants for programs designed to reduce infant mortality rates, as well as for other primary health care programs provided in designated "health-shortage" areas.
Restrictions: Only states, local governments and nonprofit organizations within health-shortage areas may apply
$ Given: Range of $15,000 - $250,000 per award; average award is $67,040 (national figures)
Number of Awards: In FY90, 11 projects were funded
Application Information: Submit inquiries to the regional office address above
Deadline: Varies; contact local office for dates
National Contact: Executive Director, Appalachian Regional Commission, (202) 673-7874
Local Contact: Director, Department of Economic and Community Affairs

Department of Health and Human Services, Region IV Office
101 Marietta Tower
Suite 1515
Atlanta, GA 30323
(404) 331-2442

Programs: See the Federal Grants chapter for the following listings:
• Community Health Centers
• Migrant Health Centers Grants
• Administration on Developmental Disabilities—Basic Support and Advocacy Grants
• Maternal and Child Health-Targeted Infant Mortality Initiative
Contact: Earl Forsythe

ALASKA

Department of Health and Human Services, Region X Office
2201 Sixth Avenue
RX-01
Seattle, WA 98121
(206) 553-0420

Programs: See the Federal Grants chapter for the following listings:
• Community Health Centers
• Migrant Health Centers Grants
• Administration on Developmental Disabilities—Basic Support and Advocacy Grants
• Maternal and Child Health-Targeted Infant Mortality Initiative
Contact: Elizabeth G. Healy

STATE AND REGIONAL GOVERNMENT GRANTS

• •

Alaska Area Native Health Service
P.O. Box 107741
Anchorage, AK 99510
(907) 257-1153

Program: Indian Health Service—Health Management Development Program
(Federal program 93.228)
Description: Project grants for American Indian/Native Alaskan projects designed to provide a full range of curative, preventive and rehabilitative health services. Assistance to federally-recognized tribes and tribal organizations. Designed to increase the capability of American Indians and Native Alaskans to manage their own health programs.
Restrictions: Only federally-recognized tribes and tribal organizations may apply
$ Given: Range of $6,250 - $6.3 million per project; average award is $62,693 (national figures)
Number of Awards: Approximately 100 awards made annually nationwide
Application Information: Contact local Health Service office for standard application forms
Deadline: Some grant applications must be submitted 90 days prior to proposed project start date; others have specific deadlines. Contact local Health Service office for current deadline information.
National Contacts: Kay Carpentier, grants management contact, (301) 443-5204; or B. Bowman, program contact, (301) 443-6840
Local Contact: Gerald Ivey

ARIZONA

Department of Health and Human Services, Region IX Office
Federal Office Building
50 United Nations Plaza
Room 431
San Francisco, CA 94102
(415) 556-1961

Programs: See the Federal Grants chapter for the following listings:
• Community Health Centers
• Migrant Health Centers Grants
• Administration on Developmental Disabilities—Basic Support and Advocacy Grants
• Maternal and Child Health-Targeted Infant Mortality Initiative
Contact: Emory Lee

Phoenix Area Indian Health Service
3738 North 16th Street
Suite A
Phoenix, AZ 85016-5981
(602) 241-2052
Contact: Don J. Davis

and
Navajo Area Indian Health Service
P.O. Box G
Window Rock, AZ 86515
(602) 871-5811

and
Tucson Area Indian Health Service
7900 South J. Stock Road
Tucson, AZ 85746-9352
(602) 629-6600
Contact: Eleanore Robertson

Program: Indian Health Service—Health Management Development Program (Federal program 93.228)
Description: Project grants for American Indian projects designed to provide a full range of curative, preventive and rehabilitative health services. Assistance to federally-recognized tribes and tribal organizations. Designed to increase the capability of American Indians to manage their own health programs.
Restrictions: Only federally-recognized tribes and tribal organizations may apply
$ Given: Range of $6,250 - $6.3 million per project; average award is $62,693 (national figures)
Number of Awards: Approximately 100 awards made annually nationwide
Application Information: Contact local Health Service office for standard application forms
Deadline: Some grant applications must be submitted 90 days prior to proposed project start date; others have specific deadlines. Contact your local Health Service office.
National Contacts: Kay Carpenter, grants management contact, (301) 443-5204; or B. Bowman, program contact, (301) 443-6840

ARKANSAS

Department of Health and Human Services, Region VI Office
1200 Main Tower Building
Room 1100
Dallas, TX 75202
(214) 767-3301

Programs: See the Federal Grants chapter for the following listings:
• Community Health Centers
• Migrant Health Centers Grants
• Administration on Developmental Disabilities—Basic Support and Advocacy Grants
• Maternal and Child Health-Targeted Infant Mortality Initiative
Contact: J.B. Keith

CALIFORNIA

Department of Health and Human Services, Region IX Office
Federal Office Building
50 United Nations Plaza
Room 431
San Francisco, CA 94102
(415) 556-1961

Programs: See the Federal Grants chapter for the following listings:
• Community Health Centers
• Migrant Health Centers Grants
• Administration on Developmental Disabilities—Basic Support and Advocacy Grants
• Maternal and Child Health-Targeted Infant Mortality Initiative
Contact: Emory Lee

• • • • • • • • • • • • • • • • • • •

California Area Indian Health Service
2999 Fulton Avenue
Sacramento, CA 95821
(916) 978-4202

Program: Indian Health Service—Health Management Development Program (Federal program 93.228)
Description: Project grants for American Indian projects designed to provide a full range of curative, preventive and rehabilitative health services. Assistance to federally-recognized tribes and tribal organizations. Designed to increase the capability of American Indians to manage their own health programs.
Restrictions: Only federally-recognized tribes and tribal organizations may apply
$ Given: Range of $6,250 - $6.3 million per project; average award is $62,693 (national figures)
Number of Awards: Approximately 100 awards made annually nationwide
Application Information: Contact local Health Service office for standard application forms
Deadline: Some grant applications must be submitted 90 days prior to proposed project start date; others have specific deadlines. Contact local Health Service office for current deadline information.
National Contacts: Kay Carpentier, grants management contact, (301) 443-5204; or B. Bowman, program contact, (301) 443-6840
Local Contact: T.J. Harwood

COLORADO

Department of Health and Human Services, Region VIII Office
Federal Building
Room 1185
1961 Stout Street
Denver, CO 80294-3538
(303) 844-3372

Programs: See the Federal Grants chapter for the following listings:
• Community Health Centers
• Migrant Health Centers Grants
• Administration on Developmental Disabilities—Basic Support and Advocacy Grants
• Maternal and Child Health-Targeted Infant Mortality Initiative
Contact: Paul Denham

STATE AND REGIONAL GOVERNMENT GRANTS

CONNECTICUT

Department of Health and Human Services, Region I Office
John F. Kennedy Federal Bldg.
Room 2411
Government Center
Boston, MA 02203
(617) 565-1500

Programs: See the Federal Grants chapter for the following listings:
• Community Health Centers
• Migrant Health Centers Grants
• Administration on Developmental Disabilities—Basic Support and Advocacy Grants
• Maternal and Child Health-Targeted Infant Mortality Initiative
Contact: Maureen Osolnik

DELAWARE

Department of Health and Human Services, Region III Office
3535 Market Street
Room 11480, Gateway Bldg.
Philadelphia, PA 19104
MAIL ADDRESS:
P.O. Box 13716
Mail Stop No. 1
Philadelphia, PA 19101
(215) 596-6492

Programs: See the Federal Grants chapter for the following listings:
• Community Health Centers
• Migrant Health Centers Grants
• Administration on Developmental Disabilities—Basic Support and Advocacy Grants
• Maternal and Child Health-Targeted Infant Mortality Initiative
Contact: James Mengel

DISTRICT OF COLUMBIA

Department of Health and Human Services, Region III Office
3535 Market Street, Rm. 11480
Gateway Building
Philadelphia, PA 19104
MAIL ADDRESS:
P.O. Box 13716
Mail Stop No. 1
Philadelphia, PA 19101
(215) 596-6492

Programs: See the Federal Grants chapter for the following listings:
• Community Health Centers
• Migrant Health Centers Grants
• Administration on Developmental Disabilities—Basic Support and Advocacy Grants
• Maternal and Child Health-Targeted Infant Mortality Initiative
Contact: James Mengel

STATE AND REGIONAL GOVERNMENT GRANTS

• • • • • • • • • • • • • • • • • • • •

FLORIDA

Department of Health and Human Services, Region IV Office
101 Marietta Tower
Suite 1515
Atlanta, GA 30323
(404) 331-2442

Programs: See the Federal Grants chapter for the following listings:
• Community Health Centers
• Migrant Health Centers Grants
• Administration on Developmental Disabilities—Basic Support and Advocacy Grants
• Maternal and Child Health-Targeted Infant Mortality Initiative
Contact: Earl Forsythe

GEORGIA

Appalachian Regional Commission
State Alternate's Office
1200 Equitable Building
100 Peachtree Street
Atlanta, GA 30303
(404) 656-3836

Program: Appalachian 202 Health Programs
(Federal program 23.004)
Description: Project grants for programs designed to reduce infant mortality rates, as well as for other primary health care programs provided in designated "health-shortage" areas.
Restrictions: Only states, local governments and nonprofit organizations within health-shortage areas may apply
$ Given: Range of $15,000 - $250,000 per award; average award is $67,040 (national figures)
Number of Awards: In FY90, 11 projects were funded
Application Information: Submit inquiries to the regional office address above
Deadline: Varies; contact local office for dates
National Contact: Executive Director, Appalachian Regional Commission, (202) 673-7874
Local Contact: Executive Assistant to the Commissioner

Department of Health and Human Services, Region IV Office
101 Marietta Tower
Suite 1515
Atlanta, GA 30323
(404) 331-2442

Programs: See the Federal Grants chapter for the following listings:
• Community Health Centers
• Migrant Health Centers Grants
• Administration on Developmental Disabilities—Basic Support and Advocacy Grants
• Maternal and Child Health-Targeted Infant Mortality Initiative
Contact: Earl Forsythe

HAWAII

Department of Health and Human Services, Region IX Office
Federal Office Building
50 United Nations Plaza
Room 431
San Francisco, CA 94102
(415) 556-1961

Programs: See the Federal Grants chapter for the following listings:
• Community Health Centers
• Migrant Health Centers Grants
• Administration on Developmental Disabilities—Basic Support and Advocacy Grants
• Maternal and Child Health-Targeted Infant Mortality Initiative
Contact: Emory Lee

U.S. Public Health Service
University of Hawaii
School of Public Health
1960 East-West Road
Honolulu, HI 96822
(808) 956-8914

Program: Native Hawaiian Health Centers
(Federal program 93.932)
Description: Project grants to provide primary health care services and health education to address the needs of Native Hawaiians. Emphasis on integration of traditional health concepts with western medicine to create one system of care that utilizes existing health resources to the greatest extent possible.
Restrictions: Limited to Native Hawaiian health centers, Native Hawaiian organizations, and public or nonprofit private health providers. A "Native Hawaiian" is defined as an individual who has any ancestors who were natives, prior to 1778, of the area now recognized as the State of Hawaii.
$ Given: Range of $250,000 - $600,000 per award
Number of Awards: Up to 9 grants annually
Application Information: Contact the representative at the address above for guidelines and application information
National Contacts: Program contact, Elizabeth A. Hickey, Public Health Analyst, (301) 443-8134; grants management contact, Gary Houseknecht, Grants Officer, (301) 443-5902
Local Contact: David Callagy, U.S. Public Health Service representative in Hawaii

IDAHO

Department of Health and Human Services, Region X Office
2201 Sixth Avenue
RX-01
Seattle, WA 98121
(206) 553-0420

Programs: See the Federal Grants chapter for the following listings:
• Community Health Centers
• Migrant Health Centers Grants
• Administration on Developmental Disabilities—Basic Support and Advocacy Grants
• Maternal and Child Health-Targeted Infant Mortality Initiative
Contact: Elizabeth G. Healy

STATE AND REGIONAL GOVERNMENT GRANTS

• •

ILLINOIS

Department of Health and Human Services, Region V Office
105 West Adams
23rd Floor
Chicago, IL 60603
(312) 353-5132

Programs: See the Federal Grants chapter for the following listings:
• Community Health Centers
• Migrant Health Centers Grants
• Administration on Developmental Disabilities—Basic Support and Advocacy Grants
• Maternal and Child Health-Targeted Infant Mortality Initiative
Contact: Hiroshi Kanno

INDIANA

Department of Health and Human Services, Region V Office
105 West Adams
23rd Floor
Chicago, IL 60603
(312) 353-5132

Programs: See the Federal Grants chapter for the following listings:
• Community Health Centers
• Migrant Health Centers Grants
• Administration on Developmental Disabilities—Basic Support and Advocacy Grants
• Maternal and Child Health-Targeted Infant Mortality Initiative
Contact: Hiroshi Kanno

IOWA

Department of Health and Human Services, Region VII Office
601 East 12th Street
Room 210
Kansas City, MO 64106
(816) 426-2821

Programs: See the Federal Grants chapter for the following listings:
• Community Health Centers
• Migrant Health Centers Grants
• Administration on Developmental Disabilities—Basic Support and Advocacy Grants
• Maternal and Child Health-Targeted Infant Mortality Initiative
Contact: Barbara Gumminger

KANSAS

Department of Health and Human Services, Region VII Office
601 East 12th Street
Room 210
Kansas City, MO 64106
(816) 426-2821

Programs: See the Federal Grants chapter for the following listings:
• Community Health Centers
• Migrant Health Centers Grants
• Administration on Developmental Disabilities—Basic Support and Advocacy Grants
• Maternal and Child Health-Targeted Infant Mortality Initiative
Contact: Barbara Gumminger

KENTUCKY

Appalachian Regional Commission
State Alternate's Office
Capital Plaza Tower
Frankfort, KY 40601
(502) 564-2382

Program: Appalachian 202 Health Programs (Federal program 23.004)
Description: Project grants for programs designed to reduce infant mortality rates, as well as for other primary health care programs provided in designated "health-shortage" areas.
Restrictions: Only states, local governments and nonprofit organizations within health-shortage areas may apply
$ Given: Range of $15,000 - $250,000 per award; average award is $67,040 (national figures)
Number of Awards: In FY90, 11 projects were funded
Application Information: Submit inquiries to the regional office address above
Deadline: Varies; contact local office for dates
National Contact: Executive Director, Appalachian Regional Commission, (202) 673-7874
Local Contact: Commissioner of Local Governments

Department of Health and Human Services, Region IV Office
101 Marietta Tower
Suite 1515
Atlanta, GA 30323
(404) 331-2442

Programs: See the Federal Grants chapter for the following listings:
• Community Health Centers
• Migrant Health Centers Grants
• Administration on Developmental Disabilities—Basic Support and Advocacy Grants
• Maternal and Child Health-Targeted Infant Mortality Initiative
Contact: Earl Forsythe

LOUISIANA

Department of Health and Human Services, Region VI Office
1200 Main Tower Building
Room 1100
Dallas, TX 75202
(214) 767-3301

Programs: See the Federal Grants chapter for the following listings:
• Community Health Centers
• Migrant Health Centers Grants
• Administration on Developmental Disabilities—Basic Support and Advocacy Grants
• Maternal and Child Health-Targeted Infant Mortality Initiative
Contact: J.B. Keith

STATE AND REGIONAL GOVERNMENT GRANTS

• •

MAINE

Department of Health and Human Services, Region I Office
John F. Kennedy Federal Bldg.
Room 2411
Government Center
Boston, MA 02203
(617) 565-1500

Programs: See the Federal Grants chapter for the following listings:
• Community Health Centers
• Migrant Health Centers Grants
• Administration on Developmental Disabilities—Basic Support and Advocacy Grants
• Maternal and Child Health-Targeted Infant Mortality Initiative
Contact: Maureen Osolnik

MARYLAND

Appalachian Regional Commission
State Alternate's Office
Maryland Office of Planning
Room 1101
301 West Preston Street
Baltimore, MD 21201
(301) 255-4510

Program: Appalachian 202 Health Programs (Federal program 23.004)
Description: Project grants for programs designed to reduce infant mortality rates, as well as for other primary health care programs provided in designated "health-shortage" areas.
Restrictions: Only states, local governments and nonprofit organizations within health-shortage areas may apply
$ Given: Range of $15,000 - $250,000 per award; average award is $67,040 (national figures)
Number of Awards: In FY90, 11 projects were funded
Application Information: Submit inquiries to the regional office address above
Deadline: Varies; contact local office for dates
National Contact: Executive Director, Appalachian Regional Commission, (202) 673-7874
Local Contact: Director, Maryland Office of Planning

Department of Health and Human Services, Region III Office
3535 Market Street
Room 11480, Gateway Bldg.
Philadelphia, PA 19104
MAIL ADDRESS:
P.O. Box 13716
Mail Stop No. 1
Philadelphia, PA 19101
(215) 596-6492

Programs: See the Federal Grants chapter for the following listings:
• Community Health Centers
• Migrant Health Centers Grants
• Administration on Developmental Disabilities—Basic Support and Advocacy Grants
• Maternal and Child Health-Targeted Infant Mortality Initiative
Contact: James Mengel

STATE AND REGIONAL GOVERNMENT GRANTS

MASSACHUSETTS

Department of Health and Human Services, Region I Office
John F. Kennedy Federal Bldg.
Room 2411
Government Center
Boston, MA 02203
(617) 565-1500

Programs: See the Federal Grants chapter for the following listings:
• Community Health Centers
• Migrant Health Centers Grants
• Administration on Developmental Disabilities—Basic Support and Advocacy Grants
• Maternal and Child Health-Targeted Infant Mortality Initiative
Contact: Maureen Osolnik

MICHIGAN

Department of Health and Human Services, Region V Office
105 West Adams
23rd Floor
Chicago, IL 60603
(312) 353-5132

Programs: See the Federal Grants chapter for the following listings:
• Community Health Centers
• Migrant Health Centers Grants
• Administration on Developmental Disabilities—Basic Support and Advocacy Grants
• Maternal and Child Health-Targeted Infant Mortality Initiative
Contact: Hiroshi Kanno

MINNESOTA

Department of Health and Human Services, Region V Office
105 West Adams
23rd Floor
Chicago, IL 60603
(312) 353-5132

Programs: See the Federal Grants chapter for the following listings:
• Community Health Centers
• Migrant Health Centers Grants
• Administration on Developmental Disabilities—Basic Support and Advocacy Grants
• Maternal and Child Health-Targeted Infant Mortality Initiative
Contact: Hiroshi Kanno

STATE AND REGIONAL GOVERNMENT GRANTS

· · · · · · · · · · · · · · · · · · · ·

Bemidji Area Indian Health Service
203 Federal Building
Bemidji, MN 56601
(218) 751-7701

Program: Indian Health Service—Health Management Development Program (Federal program 93.228)
Description: Program grants for American Indian projects designed to provide a full range of curative, preventive and rehabilitative health services. Assistance to federally-recognized tribes and tribal organizations. Designed to increase the capability of American Indians to manage their own health programs.
Restrictions: Only federally-recognized tribes and tribal organizations may apply
$ Given: Range of $6,250 - $6.3 million per project; average award is $62,693 (national figures)
Number of Awards: Approximately 100 awards made annually nationwide
Application Information: Contact local Health Service office for standard application forms
Deadline: Some grant applications must be submitted 90 days prior to proposed project start date; others have specific deadlines. Contact local Health Service office.
National Contacts: Kay Carpentier, grants management contact, (301) 443-5204; or B. Bowman, program contact, (301) 443-6840
Local Contact: Dr. Kathleen Annette, Director

MISSISSIPPI

Appalachian Regional Commission
State Alternate's Office
State Office of Appalachia
Box 1606
Tupelo, MS 38802
(601) 844-1184

Program: Appalachian 202 Health Programs (Federal program 23.004)
Description: Project grants for programs designed to reduce infant mortality rates, as well as for other primary health care programs provided in designated "health-shortage" areas.
Restrictions: Only states, local governments and nonprofit organizations within health-shortage areas may apply
$ Given: Range of $15,000 - $250,000 per award; average award is $67,040 (national figures)
Number of Awards: In FY90, 11 projects were funded
Application Information: Submit inquiries to the regional office address above
Deadline: Varies; contact local office for dates
National Contact: Executive Director, Appalachian Regional Commission, (202) 673-7874
Local Contact: Governor's Alternate

• •

Department of Health and Human Services, Region IV Office
101 Marietta Tower
Suite 1515
Atlanta, GA 30323
(404) 331-2442

Programs: See the Federal Grants chapter for the following listings:
• Community Health Centers
• Migrant Health Centers Grants
• Administration on Developmental Disabilities—Basic Support and Advocacy Grants
• Maternal and Child Health-Targeted Infant Mortality Initiative
Contact: Earl Forsythe

MISSOURI

Department of Health and Human Services, Region VII Office
601 East 12th Street
Room 210
Kansas City, MO 64106
(816) 426-2821

Programs: See the Federal Grants chapter for the following listings:
• Community Health Centers
• Migrant Health Centers Grants
• Administration on Developmental Disabilities—Basic Support and Advocacy Grants
• Maternal and Child Health-Targeted Infant Mortality Initiative
Contact: Barbara Gumminger

MONTANA

Department of Health and Human Services, Region VIII Office
Federal Building
Room 1185
1961 Stout Street
Denver, CO 80294-3538
(303) 844-3372

Programs: See the Federal Grants chapter for the following listings:
• Community Health Centers
• Migrant Health Centers Grants
• Administration on Developmental Disabilities—Basic Support and Advocacy Grants
• Maternal and Child Health-Targeted Infant Mortality Initiative
Contact: Paul Denham

STATE AND REGIONAL GOVERNMENT GRANTS

• • • • • • • • • • • • • • • • • • • •

**Billings Area Indian
Health Service**
711 Central Avenue
P.O. Box 2143
Billings, MT 59103
(406) 657-6403

Program: Indian Health Service—Health Management
Development Program (Federal program 93.228)
Description: Project grants for American Indian projects
designed to provide a full range of curative, preventive and
rehabilitative health services. Assistance to federally-
recognized tribes and tribal organizations. Designed to
increase the capability of American Indians to manage their
own health programs.
Restrictions: Only federally-recognized tribes and tribal
organizations may apply
$ Given: Range of $6,250 - $6.3 million per project; average
award is $62,693 (national figures)
Number of Awards: Approximately 100 awards made
annually nationwide
Application Information: Contact local Health Service office
for standard application forms
Deadline: Some grant applications must be submitted 90
days prior to proposed project start date; others have
specific deadlines. Contact local Health Service office for
current deadline information.
National Contacts: Kay Carpentier, grants management
contact, (301) 443-5204; or B. Bowman, program contact,
(301) 443-6840
Local Contact: Duane L. Jeanotte

NEBRASKA

**Department of Health and
Human Services,
Region VII Office**
601 East 12th Street
Room 210
Kansas City, MO 64106
(816) 426-2821

Programs: See the Federal Grants chapter for the following
listings:
• Community Health Centers
• Migrant Health Centers Grants
• Administration on Developmental Disabilities—Basic
Support and Advocacy Grants
• Maternal and Child Health-Targeted Infant Mortality Initiative
Contact: Barbara Gumminger

NEVADA

Department of Health and Human Services, Region IX Office
Federal Office Building
50 United Nations Plaza
Room 431
San Francisco, CA 94102
(415) 556-1961

Programs: See the Federal Grants chapter for the following listings:
• Community Health Centers
• Migrant Health Centers Grants
• Administration on Developmental Disabilities—Basic Support and Advocacy Grants
• Maternal and Child Health-Targeted Infant Mortality Initiative
Contact: Emory Lee

NEW HAMPSHIRE

Department of Health and Human Services, Region I Office
John F. Kennedy Federal Bldg.
Room 2411
Government Center
Boston, MA 02203
(617) 565-1500

Programs: See the Federal Grants chapter for the following listings:
• Community Health Centers
• Migrant Health Centers Grants
• Administration on Developmental Disabilities—Basic Support and Advocacy Grants
• Maternal and Child Health-Targeted Infant Mortality Initiative
Contact: Maureen Osolnik

NEW JERSEY

Department of Health and Human Services, Region II Office
26 Federal Plaza
Room 3835
New York, NY 10278
(212) 264-4600

Programs: See the Federal Grants chapter for the following listings:
• Community Health Centers
• Migrant Health Centers Grants
• Administration on Developmental Disabilities—Basic Support and Advocacy Grants
• Maternal and Child Health-Targeted Infant Mortality Initiative
Contact: Kathleen Harten

NEW MEXICO

Department of Health and Human Services, Region VI Office
1200 Main Tower Building
Room 1100
Dallas, TX 75202
(214) 767-3301

Programs: See the Federal Grants chapter for the following listings:
• Community Health Centers
• Migrant Health Centers Grants
• Administration on Developmental Disabilities—Basic Support and Advocacy Grants
• Maternal and Child Health-Targeted Infant Mortality Initiative
Contact: J.B. Keith

STATE AND REGIONAL GOVERNMENT GRANTS

. . . .

Albuquerque Area Indian Health Service
Headquarters West Indian Health Service
Federal Office Building and U.S. Courthouse
505 Marquette Avenue, N.W. Suite 1502
Albuquerque, NM 87102-2162
(505) 766-2151

Program: Indian Health Service—Health Management Development Program (Federal program 93.228)
Description: Project grants for American Indian projects designed to provide a full range of curative, preventive and rehabilitative health services. Assistance to federally-recognized tribes and tribal organizations. Designed to increase the capability of American Indians to manage their own health programs.
Restrictions: Only federally-recognized tribes and tribal organizations may apply
$ Given: Range of $6,250 - $6.3 million per project; average award is $62,693 (national figures)
Number of Awards: Approximately 100 awards made annually nationwide
Application Information: Contact local Health Service office for standard application forms
Deadline: Some grant applications must be submitted 90 days prior to proposed project start date; others have specific deadlines. Contact local Health Service office for current deadline information.
National Contacts: Kay Carpentier, grants management contact, (301) 443-5204; or B. Bowman, program contact, (301) 443-6840
Local Contact: Eleanore Robertson

NEW YORK

Appalachian Regional Commission
State Alternate's Office
Department of State
162 Washington Avenue
Albany, NY 12231
(518) 474-4750

Program: Appalachian 202 Health Programs (Federal program 23.004)
Description: Project grants for programs designed to reduce infant mortality rates, as well as for other primary health care programs provided in designated "health-shortage" areas.
Restrictions: Only states, local governments and nonprofit organizations within health-shortage areas may apply
$ Given: Range of $15,000 - $250,000 per award; average award is $67,040 (national figures)
Number of Awards: In FY90, 11 projects were funded
Application Information: Submit inquiries to the regional office address above
Deadline: Varies; contact local office for dates
National Contact: Executive Director, Appalachian Regional Commission, (202) 673-7874
Local Contact: Secretary of State

Department of Health and Human Services, Region II Office
26 Federal Plaza
Room 3835
New York, NY 10278
(212) 264-4600

Programs: See the Federal Grants chapter for the following listings:
• Community Health Centers
• Migrant Health Centers Grants
• Administration on Developmental Disabilities—Basic Support and Advocacy Grants
• Maternal and Child Health-Targeted Infant Mortality Initiative
Contact: Kathleen Harten

NORTH CAROLINA

Appalachian Regional Commission
State Alternate's Office
Department of Administration
116 West Jones Street
Raleigh, NC 27611
(919) 733-7232

Program: Appalachian 202 Health Programs (Federal program 23.004)
Description: Project grants for programs designed to reduce infant mortality rates, as well as for other primary health care programs provided in designated "health-shortage" areas.
Restrictions: Only states, local governments and nonprofit organizations within health-shortage areas may apply
$ Given: Range of $15,000 - $250,000 per award; average award is $67,040 (national figures)
Number of Awards: In FY90, 11 projects were funded
Application Information: Submit inquiries to the regional office address above
Deadline: Varies; contact local office for dates
National Contact: Executive Director, Appalachian Regional Commission, (202) 673-7874
Local Contact: Secretary, Department of Administration

Department of Health and Human Services, Region IV Office
101 Marietta Tower
Suite 1515
Atlanta, GA 30323
(404) 331-2442

Programs: See the Federal Grants chapter for the following listings:
• Community Health Centers
• Migrant Health Centers Grants
• Administration on Developmental Disabilities—Basic Support and Advocacy Grants
• Maternal and Child Health-Targeted Infant Mortality Initiative
Contact: Earl Forsythe

STATE AND REGIONAL GOVERNMENT GRANTS

. . . .

NORTH DAKOTA

Department of Health and Human Services, Region VIII Office
Federal Building
Room 1185
1961 Stout Street
Denver, CO 80294-3538
(303) 844-3372

Programs: See the Federal Grants chapter for the following listings:
• Community Health Centers
• Migrant Health Centers Grants
• Administration on Developmental Disabilities—Basic Support and Advocacy Grants
• Maternal and Child Health-Targeted Infant Mortality Initiative
Contact: Paul Denham

OHIO

Appalachian Regional Commission
State Alternate's Office
Governor's Office of Appalachia
77 South High Street
Columbus, OH 43266-0101
(614) 644-9228

Program: Appalachian 202 Health Programs (Federal program 23.004)
Description: Project grants for programs designed to reduce infant mortality rates, as well as for other primary health care programs provided in designated "health-shortage" areas.
Restrictions: Only states, local governments and nonprofit organizations within health-shortage areas may apply
$ Given: Range of $15,000 - $250,000 per award; average award is $67,040 (national figures)
Number of Awards: In FY90, 11 projects were funded
Application Information: Submit inquiries to the regional office address above
Deadline: Varies; contact local office for dates
National Contact: Executive Director, Appalachian Regional Commission, (202) 673-7874
Local Contact: Director, Governor's Office of Appalachia

Department of Health and Human Services, Region V Office
105 West Adams
23rd Floor
Chicago, IL 60603
(312) 353-5132

Programs: See the Federal Grants chapter for the following listings:
• Community Health Centers
• Migrant Health Centers Grants
• Administration on Developmental Disabilities—Basic Support and Advocacy Grants
• Maternal and Child Health-Targeted Infant Mortality Initiative
Contact: Hiroshi Kanno

. . . .

OKLAHOMA

Department of Health and Human Services, Region VI Office
1200 Main Tower Building
Room 1100
Dallas, TX 75202
(214) 767-3301

Programs: See the Federal Grants chapter for the following listings:
• Community Health Centers
• Migrant Health Centers Grants
• Administration on Developmental Disabilities—Basic Support and Advocacy Grants
• Maternal and Child Health-Targeted Infant Mortality Initiative
Contact: J.B. Keith

Oklahoma City Area Indian Health Service
215 Dean A. McGee Street, N.W.
Oklahoma City, OK 73102-3477
(405) 237-4796

Program: Indian Health Service—Health Management Development Program (Federal program 93.228)
Description: Project grants for American Indian projects designed to provide a full range of curative, preventive and rehabilitative health services. Assistance to federally-recognized tribes and tribal organizations. Designed to increase the capability of American Indians to manage their own health programs.
Restrictions: Only federally-recognized tribes and tribal organizations may apply
$ Given: Range of $6,250 - $6.3 million per project; average award is $62,693 (national figures)
Number of Awards: Approximately 100 awards made annually nationwide
Application Information: Contact local Health Service office for standard application forms
Deadline: Some grant applications must be submitted 90 days prior to proposed project start date; others have specific deadlines. Contact local Health Service office for current deadline information.
National Contacts: Kay Carpentier, grants management contact, (301) 443-5204; or B. Bowman, (301) 443-6840
Local Contact: Dr. Robert Harry, Director

OREGON

Department of Health and Human Services, Region X Office
2201 Sixth Avenue
RX-01
Seattle, WA 98121
(206) 553-0420

Programs: See the Federal Grants chapter for the following listings:
• Community Health Centers
• Migrant Health Centers Grants
• Administration on Developmental Disabilities—Basic Support and Advocacy Grants
• Maternal and Child Health-Targeted Infant Mortality Initiative
Contact: Elizabeth G. Healy

STATE AND REGIONAL GOVERNMENT GRANTS

• • • • • • • • • • • • • • • • • •

Portland Area Indian Health Service
1220 S.W. Third Avenue
Room 476
Portland, OR 97204-2892
(503) 221-2020

Program: Indian Health Service—Health Management Development Program (Federal program 93.228)
Description: Project grants for American Indian projects designed to provide a full range of curative, preventive and rehabilitative health services. Assistance to federally-recognized tribes and tribal organizations. Designed to increase the capability of American Indians to manage their own health programs.
Restrictions: Only federally-recognized tribes and tribal organizations may apply
$ Given: Range of $6,250 - $6.3 million per project; average award is $62,693 (national figures)
Number of Awards: Approximately 100 awards made annually nationwide
Application Information: Contact local Health Service office for standard application forms
Deadline: Some grant applications must be submitted 90 days prior to proposed project start date; others have specific deadlines. Contact local Health Service office for current deadline information.
National Contacts: Kay Carpentier, grants management contact, (301) 443-5204; or B. Bowman, program contact, (301) 443-6840
Local Contact: Dr. Terrance Batliner, Director

PENNSYLVANIA

Appalachian Regional Commission
State Alternate's Office
433 Forum Building
Harrisburg, PA 17120
(717) 787-3840

Program: Appalachian 202 Health Programs (Federal program 23.004)
Description: Project grants for programs designed to reduce infant mortality rates, as well as for other primary health care programs provided in designated "health-shortage" areas.
Restrictions: Only states, local governments and nonprofit organizations within health-shortage areas may apply
$ Given: Range of $15,000 - $250,000 per award; average award is $67,040 (national figures)
Number of Awards: In FY90, 11 projects were funded
Application Information: Submit inquiries to the regional office address above
Deadline: Varies; contact local office for dates
National Contact: Executive Director, Appalachian Regional Commission, (202) 673-7874
Local Contact: Secretary of Commerce

Department of Health and Human Services, Region III Office

3535 Market Street
Room 11480, Gateway Bldg.
Philadelphia, PA 19104
MAIL ADDRESS:
P.O. Box 13716, Mail Stop #1
Philadelphia, PA 19101
(215) 596-6492

Programs: See the Federal Grants chapter for the following listings:
• Community Health Centers
• Migrant Health Centers Grants
• Administration on Developmental Disabilities—Basic Support and Advocacy Grants
• Maternal and Child Health-Targeted Infant Mortality Initiative
Contact: James Mengel

RHODE ISLAND

Department of Health and Human Services, Region I Office

John F. Kennedy Federal Bldg.
Room 2411
Government Center
Boston, MA 02203
(617) 565-1500

Programs: See the Federal Grants chapter for the following listings:
• Community Health Centers
• Migrant Health Centers Grants
• Administration on Developmental Disabilities—Basic Support and Advocacy Grants
• Maternal and Child Health-Targeted Infant Mortality Initiative
Contact: Maureen Osolnik

SOUTH CAROLINA

Appalachian Regional Commission

State Alternate's Office
South Carolina Washington Office
Office of the Governor
444 North Capitol Street
Suite 234
Washington, DC 20001
(202) 624-7784

Program: Appalachian 202 Health Programs (Federal program 23.004)
Description: Project grants for programs designed to reduce infant mortality rates, as well as for other primary health care programs provided in designated "health-shortage" areas.
Restrictions: Only states, local governments and nonprofit organizations within health-shortage areas may apply
$ Given: Range of $15,000 - $250,000 per award; average award is $67,040 (national figures)
Number of Awards: In FY90, 11 projects were funded
Application Information: Submit inquiries to the regional office address above
Deadline: Varies; contact local office for dates
National Contact: Executive Director, Appalachian Regional Commission, (202) 673-7874
Local Contact: Executive Assistant, Office of the Governor

STATE AND REGIONAL GOVERNMENT GRANTS

. . . .

Department of Health and Human Services, Region IV Office
101 Marietta Tower
Suite 1515
Atlanta, GA 30323
(404) 331-2442

Programs: See the Federal Grants chapter for the following listings:
• Community Health Centers
• Migrant Health Centers Grants
• Administration on Developmental Disabilities—Basic Support and Advocacy Grants
• Maternal and Child Health-Targeted Infant Mortality Initiative
Contact: Earl Forsythe

SOUTH DAKOTA

Department of Health and Human Services, Region VIII Office
Federal Building
Room 1185
1961 Stout Street
Denver, CO 80294-3538
(303) 844-3372

Programs: See the Federal Grants chapter for the following listings:
• Community Health Centers
• Migrant Health Centers Grants
• Administration on Developmental Disabilities—Basic Support and Advocacy Grants
• Maternal and Child Health-Targeted Infant Mortality Initiative
Contact: Paul Denham

Aberdeen Area Indian Health Service
Federal Building
115 - 4th Avenue, S.E.
Aberdeen, SD 57401
(605) 226-7581

Program: Indian Health Service—Health Management Development Program (Federal program 93.228)
Description: Project grants for American Indian projects designed to provide a full range of curative, preventive and rehabilitative health services. Assistance to federally-recognized tribes and tribal organizations. Designed to increase the capability of American Indians to manage their own health programs.
Restrictions: Only federally-recognized tribes and tribal organizations may apply
$ Given: Range of $6,250 - $6.3 million per project; average award is $62,693 (national figures)
Number of Awards: Approximately 100 awards made annually nationwide
Application Information: Contact local Health Service office for standard application forms
Deadline: Some grant applications must be submitted 90 days prior to proposed project start date; others have specific deadlines. Contact your local Health Service office.
National Contacts: Kay Carpentier, grants management contact, (301) 443-5204; or B. Bowman, (301) 443-6840
Local Contact: Terrence Sloan, M.D.

STATE AND REGIONAL GOVERNMENT GRANTS

TENNESSEE

Appalachian Regional Commission
State Alternate's Office
Community Development Division
Rachel Jackson State Office Building
320 Sixth Avenue, North
Nashville, TN 37243-0405
(615) 741-2373

Program: Appalachian 202 Health Programs (Federal program 23.004)
Description: Project grants for programs designed to reduce infant mortality rates, as well as for other primary health care programs provided in designated "health-shortage" areas.
Restrictions: Only states, local governments and nonprofit organizations within health-shortage areas may apply
$ Given: Range of $15,000 - $250,000 per award; average award is $67,040 (national figures)
Number of Awards: In FY90, 11 projects were funded
Application Information: Submit inquiries to the regional office address above
Deadline: Varies; contact local office for dates
National Contact: Executive Director, Appalachian Regional Commission, (202) 673-7874
Local Contact: Assistant Commissioner, Community Development Division

Department of Health and Human Services, Region IV Office
101 Marietta Tower
Suite 1515
Atlanta, GA 30323
(404) 331-2442

Programs: See the Federal Grants chapter for the following listings:
• Community Health Centers
• Migrant Health Centers Grants
• Administration on Developmental Disabilities—Basic Support and Advocacy Grants
• Maternal and Child Health-Targeted Infant Mortality Initiative
Contact: Earl Forsythe

STATE AND REGIONAL GOVERNMENT GRANTS

• • • • • • • • • • • • • • • • • • • •

**Nashville Area Indian
Health Service**
3310 Perimeter Hill Drive
Nashville, TN 37211
(615) 736-5104

Program: Indian Health Service—Health Management
Development Program (Federal program 93.228)
Description: Project grants for American Indian projects
designed to provide a full range of curative, preventive and
rehabilitative health services. Assistance to federally-
recognized tribes and tribal organizations. Designed to
increase the capability of American Indians to manage their
own health programs.
Restrictions: Only federally-recognized tribes and tribal
organizations may apply
$ Given: Range of $6,250 - $6.3 million per project; average
award is $62,693 (national figures)
Number of Awards: Approximately 100 awards made
annually nationwide
Application Information: Contact local Health Service office
for standard application forms
Deadline: Some grant applications must be submitted 90
days prior to proposed project start date; others have
specific deadlines. Contact local Health Service office for
current deadline information.
National Contacts: Kay Carpentier, grants management
contact, (301) 443-5204; or B. Bowman, (301) 443-6840
Local Contact: James Meredith

TEXAS

**Department of Health and
Human Services,
Region VI Office**
1200 Main Tower Building
Room 1100
Dallas, TX 75202
(214) 767-3301

Programs: See the Federal Grants chapter for the following
listings:
• Community Health Centers
• Migrant Health Centers Grants
• Administration on Developmental Disabilities—Basic
Support and Advocacy Grants
• Maternal and Child Health-Targeted Infant Mortality Initiative
Contact: J.B. Keith

UTAH

**Department of Health and
Human Services,
Region VIII Office**
Federal Building, Room 1185
1961 Stout Street
Denver, CO 80294-3538
(303) 844-3372

Programs: See the Federal Grants chapter for the following
listings:
• Community Health Centers
• Migrant Health Centers Grants
• Administration on Developmental Disabilities—Basic
Support and Advocacy Grants
• Maternal and Child Health-Targeted Infant Mortality Initiative
Contact: Paul Denham

STATE AND REGIONAL GOVERNMENT GRANTS

• •

VERMONT

Department of Health and Human Services, Region I Office
John F. Kennedy Federal Building
Room 2411
Government Center
Boston, MA 02203
(617) 565-1500

Programs: See the Federal Grants chapter for the following listings:
• Community Health Centers
• Migrant Health Centers Grants
• Administration on Developmental Disabilities—Basic Support and Advocacy Grants
• Maternal and Child Health-Targeted Infant Mortality Initiative
Contact: Maureen Osolnik

VIRGINIA

Appalachian Regional Commission
State Alternate's Office
Department of Housing & Community Development
205 North Fourth Street
Richmond, VA 23219
(804) 786-1575

Program: Appalachian 202 Health Programs (Federal program 23.004)
Description: Project grants for programs designed to reduce infant mortality rates, as well as for other primary health care programs provided in designated "health-shortage" areas.
Restrictions: Only states, local governments and nonprofit organizations within health-shortage areas may apply
$ Given: Range of $15,000 - $250,000 per award; average award is $67,040 (national figures)
Number of Awards: In FY90, 11 projects were funded
Application Information: Submit inquiries to the regional office address above
Deadline: Varies; contact local office for dates
National Contact: Executive Director, Appalachian Regional Commission, (202) 673-7874
Local Contact: Director, Department of Housing & Community Development

Department of Health and Human Services, Region III Office
3535 Market Street
Room 11480, Gateway Bldg.
Philadelphia, PA 19104
MAIL ADDRESS:
P.O. Box 13716, Mail Stop #1
Philadelphia, PA 19101
(215) 596-6492

Programs: See the Federal Grants chapter for the following listings:
• Community Health Centers
• Migrant Health Centers Grants
• Administration on Developmental Disabilities—Basic Support and Advocacy Grants
• Maternal and Child Health-Targeted Infant Mortality Initiative
Contact: James Mengel

STATE AND REGIONAL GOVERNMENT GRANTS

• •

WASHINGTON

Department of Health and Human Services, Region X Office
2201 Sixth Avenue
RX-01
Seattle, WA 98121
(206) 553-0420

Programs: See the Federal Grants chapter for the following listings:
• Community Health Centers
• Migrant Health Centers Grants
• Administration on Developmental Disabilities—Basic Support and Advocacy Grants
• Maternal and Child Health-Targeted Infant Mortality Initiative
Contact: Elizabeth G. Healy

WEST VIRGINIA

Appalachian Regional Commission
State Alternate's Office
Governor's Office of Community & Industrial Development
Building 1
Room M-146
State Capitol Complex
Charleston, WV 25305
(304) 348-0400

Program: Appalachian 202 Health Programs (Federal program 23.004)
Description: Project grants for programs designed to reduce infant mortality rates, as well as for other primary health care programs provided in designated "health-shortage" areas.
Restrictions: Only states, local governments and nonprofit organizations within health-shortage areas may apply
$ Given: Range of $15,000 - $250,000 per award; average award is $67,040 (national figures)
Number of Awards: In FY90, 11 projects were funded
Application Information: Submit inquiries to the regional office address above
Deadline: Varies; contact local office for dates
National Contact: Executive Director, Appalachian Regional Commission, (202) 673-7874
Local Contact: Director, Governor's Office of Community & Industrial Development

Department of Health and Human Services, Region III Office
3535 Market Street
Room 11480, Gateway Bldg.
Philadelphia, PA 19104
MAIL ADDRESS: P.O. Box 13716, Mail Stop No. 1, Philadelphia, PA 19101
(215) 596-6492

Programs: See the Federal Grants chapter for the following listings:
• Community Health Centers
• Migrant Health Centers Grants
• Administration on Developmental Disabilities—Basic Support and Advocacy Grants
• Maternal and Child Health-Targeted Infant Mortality Initiative
Contact: James Mengel

WISCONSIN

Department of Health and Human Services, Region V Office
105 West Adams
23rd Floor
Chicago, IL 60603
(312) 353-5132

Programs: See the Federal Grants chapter for the following listings:
• Community Health Centers
• Migrant Health Centers Grants
• Administration on Developmental Disabilities—Basic Support and Advocacy Grants
• Maternal and Child Health-Targeted Infant Mortality Initiative
Contact: Hiroshi Kanno

WYOMING

Department of Health and Human Services, Region VIII Office
Federal Building
Room 1185
1961 Stout Street
Denver, CO 80294-3538
(303) 844-3372

Programs: See the Federal Grants chapter for the following listings:
• Community Health Centers
• Migrant Health Centers Grants
• Administration on Developmental Disabilities—Basic Support and Advocacy Grants
• Maternal and Child Health-Targeted Infant Mortality Initiative
Contact: Paul Denham

PUERTO RICO

Department of Health and Human Services, Region II Office
26 Federal Plaza
Room 3835
New York, NY 10278
(212) 264-4600

Programs: See the Federal Grants chapter for the following listings:
• Community Health Centers
• Migrant Health Centers Grants
• Administration on Developmental Disabilities—Basic Support and Advocacy Grants
• Maternal and Child Health-Targeted Infant Mortality Initiative
Contact: Kathleen Harten

VIRGIN ISLANDS

Department of Health and Human Services, Region II Office
26 Federal Plaza
Room 3835
New York, NY 10278
(212) 264-4600

Programs: See the Federal Grants chapter for the following listings:
• Community Health Centers
• Migrant Health Centers Grants
• Administration on Developmental Disabilities—Basic Support and Advocacy Grants
• Maternal and Child Health-Targeted Infant Mortality Initiative
Contact: Kathleen Harten

Federal Grants

The following chapter includes a limited number of
health-related financial assistance programs funded by
the federal government. Some of these listings (those
designated with •) are detailed descriptions of federal
programs administered through the regional offices
listed in the previous chapter. If one of these programs
seems appropriate for your funding needs, please refer
back to the previous chapter, "State and Regional
Government Grants," for the address of your regional
Department of Health and Human Services office.

**Individuals cannot apply directly to these sources for
funding.** The grant programs listed in this chapter
require that a nonprofit organization, community-based
organization, government agency, or tribal organization
be the direct recipient of funds. In order to receive
financial support from these federal sources, you must
work through a sponsor organization. This is a form of
flow-through funding; for a detailed discussion of how
and why to find a nonprofit sponsor, please see the
introduction to the "Flow-Through Funding" chapter.

Remember, federal grant sources are not as narrowly
defined in purpose or as accessible as private sector
funders. Often, however, the dollar amounts are larger
and worth the trouble.

Although you cannot make a direct application to any
of the sources in this chapter, your background work
can be of immense help to your sponsor organization.
Use the information provided in this chapter to identify
funding programs that seem to address your specific
situation. Make a list of what it is you need monies for
(i.e., hospital bills, long-term care costs, loss of income

• • • • • • • • • • • • • • • • • • • •

replacement). Ask yourself such questions as, are there demonstrated financial needs on the part of the patient or the patient's family? In this fashion, you can be ready to address every issue leading to support and aid in one telephone call — by being able to describe precisely the kinds of funding for which you may be eligible.

Next, call the potential funding sources and ask this: "What types of funding programs do you provide?" If the response does not include a program that meets your particular needs, ask more specific questions. **Make it clear that you have a sponsor arrangement with an appropriate organization.** If the agency you call does not offer a program to meet your needs, someone there may be able to direct you to an agency that does. If the agency publishes materials describing its funding programs, request that these be mailed to you, along with an application. Also make sure to find out if there is a deadline coming up, so that you and your sponsor will be able to return any applications by that time.

. . . .

AIDS-RELATED FUNDING

ACQUIRED IMMUNODEFICIENCY SYNDROME (AIDS) ACTIVITY

GRANTS MANAGEMENT
Grants Management Branch,
Procurement and Grants Office,
Centers for Disease Control,
Public Health Service,
Department of Health and
Human Services,
255 E. Paces Ferry Road, N.E.
Atlanta, GA 30305
(404) 842-6640

Program: Acquired Immunodeficiency Syndrome (AIDS) Activity (Federal program 93.118)

Description: Project grants for the development and implementation of HIV-related activities (surveillance, research, health education, and risk reduction). Emphasis on high-impact communities.

Restrictions: Public and private organizations (both nonprofit and for-profit), state and local governments, U.S. Territories and possessions, and small and minority-owned businesses may apply

$ Given: Range of $20,000 - $2.75 million per award; average award is $300,000 (national figures)

Number of Awards: N/A

Application Information: Forms may be obtained from the office address above

Deadline: Contact the office above for current deadline information

Contact: Edwin Lin Dixon

FEDERAL GRANTS

• •

• GRANTS TO PROVIDE OUTPATIENT EARLY INTERVENTION SERVICES WITH RESPECT TO HIV DISEASE

PROGRAM HEADQUARTERS
Division of Special Population Program Development,
Bureau of Health Care Delivery and Assistance,
Health Resources and Services Administration,
Public Health Service,
Room 7A22
Parklawn Building
Rockville, MD 20857
(301) 443-8134
Contact: Joan Holloway, Director

and

GRANTS MANAGEMENT
Bureau of Health Care Delivery and Assistance,
Health Resources and Services Administration,
Public Health Service,
12100 Parklawn Drive
Rockville, MD 20857
(301) 443-5902
Contact: Gary Houseknecht, Grants Management Officer

Program: Grants to Provide Outpatient Early Intervention Services with Respect to HIV Disease
(Federal program 93.918)
Description: Project grants to allow entities that provide primary care services to HIV-infected persons to improve the availability, accessibility, and organization of the ambulatory health services they provide. Early intervention services include: counseling and testing, risk reduction, transmission prevention, primary care diagnostic and treatment services, and case management.
Restrictions: Public and private nonprofit entities—such as migrant health centers, community health centers, family planning programs, hemophilia diagnostic and treatment centers, and other comprehensive primary care providers—may apply
$ Given: Range of $200,000 - $600,000 per award (national figures)
Number of Awards: N/A
Application Information: Program guidelines may be obtained from Program Headquarters; for information about funding within your state, contact your regional Department of Health and Human Services office (see previous chapter)
Deadline: Contact Program Headquarters or regional DHHS office for current deadline information

• •

• **HEALTH SERVICES DELIVERY TO PERSONS WITH AIDS—
DEMONSTRATION GRANTS**

**PROGRAM
HEADQUARTERS**
Division of HIV Services
Bureau of Health Resources
Development,
Health Resources and
Services Administration,
Public Health Service,
Department of Health and
Human Services,
Room 9A-05
5600 Fishers Lane
Rockville, MD 20857
(301) 443-0652
Contact: June Horner

and

GRANTS MANAGEMENT
Grants Management Branch,
Office of Program Support,
Bureau of Health Resources
Department,
Health Resources and
Services Administration,
Public Health Service,
Department of Health and
Human Services,
Parklawn Building
Room 13A38 Twinbrook
Parkway
Suite 100A
Rockville, MD 20857
(301) 443-2280
Contact: Glenna Wilcom,
Grants Management Officer

Program: AIDS Service Demonstration Projects
(Federal program 93.133)
Description: Project grants for the development and
improvement of community-based medical and social
services for individuals with AIDS and AIDS-related
conditions. Grants are for demonstration projects in
Standard Metropolitan Statistical Areas (SMSAs) with high
concentrations of individuals with AIDS.
Restrictions: Public and private entities are eligible for
funding (state and local governments, nonprofit and for-
profit organizations); applicants must be capable of
providing services to all AIDS-infected persons within SMSA
$ Given: Range of $211,700 - $1,735,000 per award; average
award is $706,000 (national figures)
Number of Awards: In FY90, 23 continuation grants were
awarded
Application Information: Program guidelines may be
obtained from Program Headquarters; for information about
funding within your state, contact your regional Department
of Health and Human Services office (see previous chapter)
Deadline: Contact Program Headquarters or regional DHHS
office for current deadline information

FEDERAL GRANTS

. . . .

HIV CARE FORMULA GRANTS

PROGRAM
HEADQUARTERS
Division of HIV Services,
Bureau of Health Resources
Development,
Health Resources and
Services Administration,
Room 9A-05
Parklawn Building
5600 Fishers Lane
Rockville, MD 20857
(301) 443-6745
Contact: G. Stephen Bowen,
MD, MPH, Director

and

GRANTS MANAGEMENT
Grants Management Branch,
Office of Program Support,
Bureau of Health Resources
and Services Administration,
Room 13A38
Parklawn Building
5600 Fishers Lane
Rockville, MD 20857
(301) 443-2280
Contact: Glenna Wilcom,
Grants Management Officer

Program: HIV Care Formula Grants
(Federal program 93.917)
Description: Formula grants to enable states to establish
and operate HIV care consortia to provide a comprehensive
continuum of care to individuals and families with HIV.
Includes home- and community-based health care services,
assured continuity of health insurance coverage, and life-
prolonging treatment. Not less than 15% of a state's funds
must be allocated for health and support services for
infants, children, women, and families with HIV.
Restrictions: U.S. states and Territories may apply
$ Given: Range of $100,000 - $13.8 million per award;
average award is $1.58 million (national figures)
Number of Awards: N/A
Application Information: Write to Grants Management
Branch for guidelines
Deadline: Contact Program Headquarters for current
deadline information

HIV EMERGENCY RELIEF FORMULA GRANTS

PROGRAM HEADQUARTERS
Division of HIV Services,
Bureau of Health Resources Development,
Health Resources and Services Administration,
Public Health Service,
Parklawn Building
Room 9A-05
5600 Fishers Lane
Rockville, MD 20857
(301) 443-6745
Contact: G. Stephen Bowen, MD, MPH, Director

and

GRANTS MANAGEMENT
Division of Grants Management,
Office of Program Support,
Bureau of Health Resources Development,
Health Resources and Services Administration,
Public Health Service,
Parklawn Building
Room 13A38
Rockville, MD 20857
(301) 443-2280
Contact: Glenna Wilcom, Grants Management Officer

Program: HIV Emergency Relief Formula Grants (Federal program 93.915)
Description: Formula grants to provide emergency assistance to areas disproportionately affected by the HIV epidemic, to allow direct financial assistance for the delivery/enhancement of HIV-related outpatient and ambulatory health and support services. Emphasis on development of effective, cost-efficient health service delivery systems to individuals and families with HIV.
Restrictions: Limited to states and other public or private nonprofit entities serving the following metropolitan areas: Atlanta, Georgia; Boston, Massachusetts; Chicago, Illinois; Dallas, Texas; Ft. Lauderdale, Florida; Houston, Texas; Los Angeles, California; Miami, Florida; New York, New York; Newark, New Jersey; Philadelphia, Pennsylvania; San Diego, California; San Francisco, California; San Juan, Puerto Rico; and Washington, DC
$ Given: Fifty percent of the amount appropriated is disbursed to the 15 eligible metropolitan areas; the remaining 50% is disbursed as discretionary funding. Range of $858,250 - $15.8 million per award; average award is $2.7 million (national figures)
Number of Awards: N/A
Application Information: Write to Division of Grants Management for guidelines
Deadline: Contact Program Headquarters for current deadline information

FEDERAL GRANTS

• • • • • • • • • • • • • • • • • • • •

HIV EMERGENCY RELIEF PROJECT GRANTS

**PROGRAM
HEADQUARTERS**
Division of HIV Services,
Bureau of Health Resources
Development,
Health Resources and
Services Administration,
Public Health Service,
Parklawn Building
Room 9A-05
Rockville, MD 20857
(301) 443-6745
Contact: G. Stephen Bowen,
MD, MPH, Director

and

GRANTS MANAGEMENT
Grants Management Branch,
Bureau of Health Resources
Development,
Public Health Service,
Parklawn Building
Room 13A38
5600 Fishers Lane
Rockville, MD 20857
(301) 443-2280
Contact: Glenna Wilcom,
Grants Management Officer

Program: HIV Emergency Relief Project Grants
(Federal program 93.914)
Description: Project grants to provide emergency assistance
to areas disproportionately affected by the HIV epidemic, to
allow direct financial assistance for the delivery/
enhancement of HIV-related outpatient and ambulatory
health and support services, including comprehensive
treatment services. Emphasis on development of effective,
cost-efficient health service delivery systems for individuals
and families with HIV.
Restrictions: Limited to states and other public or private
nonprofit entities serving the following hard-hit metropolitan
areas: Atlanta, Georgia; Boston, Massachusetts; Chicago,
Illinois; Dallas, Texas; Ft. Lauderdale, Florida; Houston,
Texas; Los Angeles, California; Miami, Florida; New York,
New York; Newark, New Jersey; Philadelphia, Pennsylvania;
San Diego, California; San Francisco, California; San Juan,
Puerto Rico; and Washington, DC
$ Given: Range of $100,000 - $13 million per award;
average award is $1.4 million (national figures)
Number of Awards: N/A
Application Information: Write to Grants Management
Branch for details
Deadline: Contact Program Headquarters for current
deadline information

• •

HIV HOME AND COMMUNITY-BASED HEALTH SERVICES

**PROGRAM
HEADQUARTERS**
Division of HIV Services,
Bureau of Health Resources
Development,
Health Resources and
Services Administration,
Public Health Service,
Room 9A-05
Parklawn Building
5600 Fishers Lane
Rockville, MD 20857
(301) 443-0652
Contact: Sheila McCarthy

and

GRANTS MANAGEMENT
Grants Management Branch,
Office of Program Support,
Bureau of Health Resources
Development,
Health Resources and
Services Administration,
Parklawn Building
Room 13A38
5600 Fishers Lane
Rockville, MD 20857
(301) 443-2280
Contact: Glenna Wilcom,
Grants Management Officer

Program: Home Health for AIDS Patients
(Federal program 93.199)
Description: Formula grants to states, U.S. Territories and
American Indian tribes or tribal organizations to fund home
and community-based health services for HIV-infected
individuals who are either medically or chronically
dependent. Funds may be used for: durable medical
equipment; home health aide services; day treatment or
partial hospitalization; home intravenous (IV) therapy; and
routine diagnostic tests performed in the home.
Restrictions: Funds may not be used for: diagnostic tests
performed outside the home; inpatient hospitalization;
nursing facility care; or prescription drugs (other than those
administered intravenously at home). States, U.S. Territories,
and American Indian tribes and tribal organizations may
apply.
$ Given: Range of $100,000 - $2.7 million per award;
average award is $331,000 (national figures)
Number of Awards: In FY90, 57 grants were awarded
Application Information: Guidelines may be obtained from
Program Headquarters
Deadline: Contact Program Headquarters for current
deadline information

FEDERAL GRANTS

• • • • • • • • • • • • • • • • • • •

PEDIATRIC AIDS HEALTH CARE DEMONSTRATION PROGRAM

PROGRAM HEADQUARTERS
Division of Services for Children with Special Health Care Needs,
Maternal and Child Health Bureau,
Health Resources and Services Administration,
Public Health Service,
Department of Health and Human Services,
Room 9-48
5600 Fishers Lane
Rockville, MD 20857
(301) 443-9051
Contact: Beth Roy

and

GRANTS MANAGEMENT
Grants Management Branch,
Maternal and Child Health Bureau,
Health and Resources Development,
Health Resources and Services Administration,
Public Health Service,
Department of Health and Human Services,
12300 Twinbrook Parkway
Suite 100A
Rockville, MD 20852
(301) 443-1440
Contact: Waddell Avery,
Grants Management Officer

Program: Pediatric AIDS Health Care Demonstration Program (Federal program 93.153)
Description: Project grants to fund demonstration projects setting forth innovative models for pediatric AIDS intervention, and for service coordination for child-bearing women and children with AIDS. Emphasis on collaboration of local health and social service agencies, and on the use of a case management approach in providing health services to AIDS-infected children.
Restrictions: Public and private entities, nonprofit and for-profit organizations are eligible for funding
$ Given: Range of $24,275 - $1,336,500 per award; average award was $378,000 in FY90 (national figures)
Number of Awards: In FY90, 38 projects were funded; in FY91, 15 continuation grants and 28 new grants were expected to be awarded; a total of 43 grants are expected to be awarded in FY92
Application Information: Guidelines may be obtained from Program Headquarters
Deadline: Contact Program Headquarters for current deadline information

- **PREVENTION AND PRIMARY HEALTH CARE SERVICES TO PERSONS WITH HIV INFECTION AND/OR AIDS IN COMMUNITY HEALTH FACILITIES**

PROGRAM HEADQUARTERS
Division of Special Populations Program Development,
Bureau of Health Care Delivery and Assistance,
Health Resources and Services Administration,
Public Health Service,
Department of Health and Human Services,
Room 7A22
Parklawn Building
Rockville, MD 20857
(301) 443-8134
Contact: Joan Holloway, Director

and

GRANTS MANAGEMENT
Bureau of Health Care Delivery and Assistance,
Health Resources and Services Administration,
Public Health Service,
Department of Health and Human Services,
12100 Parklawn Building
Rockville, MD 20857
(301) 443-5902
Contact: Gary Houseknecht, Grants Management Officer

Program: AIDS and HIV Infection Ambulatory Services (Federal program 93.904)

Description: Project grants to support community health facilities in improving the availability, accessibility and/or organization of ambulatory health services provided to HIV-infected persons and to individuals at risk of infection. Clinical services provided will include: counseling and testing, risk reduction, transmission prevention, primary care diagnostic and treatment services, and individual case management.

Restrictions: Nonprofit public and private community health facilities may apply (includes migrant health centers, local public hospitals, and clinics)

$ Given: Range of $200,000 - $600,000 per award (national figures)

Number of Awards: In FY90, 30 grants were awarded

Application Information: Program guidelines may be obtained from Program Headquarters; for information about funding within your state, contact your regional Department of Health and Human Services office (see previous chapter)

Deadline: Contact Program Headquarters or regional DHHS office for current deadline information

FEDERAL GRANTS

. . . .

SPECIAL PROJECTS OF NATIONAL SIGNIFICANCE (SPNS)

**PROGRAM
HEADQUARTERS**
Office of the Associate
Administrator for AIDS
Health Resources and
Services Administration
Public Health Service
Parklawn Building
Room 14A-12
5600 Fishers Lane
Rockville, MD 20857
(301) 443-9976
Contact: George Sonsel

and

GRANTS MANAGEMENT
Office of Grants Management
Bureau of Health Resources
Development
Health Resources and
Services Administration
Public Health Service
Parklawn Building
Room 13A-38
5600 Fishers Lane
Rockville, MD 20857
(301) 443-2280
Contact: Neal Meyerson

Program: Special Projects of National Significance (Federal program 93.928)
Description: Project grants to improve health service delivery to individuals with HIV. (1) To reduce sociocultural, financial and logistical barriers to access to health and support services; (2) to provide advocacy services to ensure adequate and timely receipt of health and support services; (3) to fight the social isolation resulting from HIV seropositivity; (4) to integrate mental health services into primary care.
Restrictions: Public and nonprofit private entities may apply (includes community-based organizations, local and state health departments, hospitals, institutions of higher education, etc.)
$ Given: N/A
Number of Awards: Up to 16 grants anticipated in FY91
Application Information: Contact Program Headquarters for guidelines
Deadline: Contact Program Headquarters for current deadline information

• •

COMMUNITY HEALTH CENTERS

• **COMMUNITY HEALTH CENTERS**

**PROGRAM
HEADQUARTERS**
Division Primary Care
Services,
Bureau of Health Care
Delivery and Assistance,
Health Resources and
Services Administration,
Public Health Service,
Department of Health and
Human Services,
Room 7A-55
Parklawn Building
5600 Fishers Lane
Rockville, MD 20857
(301) 443-2260
Contact: Richard Bohrer,
Director

and

GRANTS MANAGEMENT
Bureau of Health Care
Delivery and Assistance,
Health Resources and
Services Administration,
Public Health Service,
Department of Health and
Human Services,
12100 Parklawn Drive
Rockville, MD 20857
(301) 443-5902
Contact: Gary Houseknecht,
Grants Management Officer

Program: Community Health Centers
(Federal program 93.224)
Description: Project grants to support the development and
operation of community health centers that provide primary
and supplemental health services to medically-underserved
populations. Priority on improving availability, accessibility
and organization within these communities. Funds may be
used for buying or modernizing buildings, as well as for
acquiring special purpose equipment.
Restrictions: Public and nonprofit private agencies,
institutions and organizations, plus a limited number of
State and local governments, may apply
$ Given: Range of $25,000 - $4 million per award; average
award is $1.2 million (national figures)
Number of Awards: Approximately 500 community health
centers are funded annually nationwide
Application Information: Program guidelines may be
obtained from Program Headquarters; for information about
funding within your state, contact your regional Department
of Health and Human Services office (see previous chapter)
Deadline: Contact Program Headquarters or regional office
for current deadline information

FEDERAL GRANTS

• •

• MIGRANT HEALTH CENTERS GRANTS

PROGRAM
HEADQUARTERS
Migrant Health Program,
Bureau of Health Care
Delivery and Assistance,
Health Resources and
Services Administration,
Public Health Service,
Department of Health and
Human Services,
Room 7A55
5600 Fishers Lane
Rockville, MD 20857
(301) 443-1153
Contact: Jack Egan, Acting
Director

and

GRANTS MANAGEMENT
Bureau of Health Care
Delivery and Assistance,
Health Resources and
Services Administration,
Public Health Service,
Department of Health and
Human Services,
12100 Parklawn Drive
Rockville, MD 20857
(301) 443-5902
Contact: Gary Houseknecht,
Grants Management Officer

Program: Migrant Health Centers Grants
(Federal program 93.246)

Description: Project grants to fund the development and
support of migrant health centers that provide accessible
primary, supplemental and environmental health services to
migrant and seasonal farm workers and their families.
Funded services include limited hospitalization benefits.

Restrictions: Public and nonprofit private entities may
apply; priority to community-based organizations that are
representative of the population to be served

$ Given: Range of $30,000 - $1.3 million per award;
average award is $300,000 (national figures)

Number of Awards: Approximately 100 centers are funded
annually nationwide

Application Information: Program guidelines may be
obtained from Program Headquarters; for information about
funding within your state, contact your regional Department
of Health and Human Services office (see previous chapter)

Deadline: Contact Program Headquarters or regional office
for current deadline information

. . . .

RURAL HEALTH SERVICES OUTREACH

PROGRAM HEADQUARTERS

Office of Rural Health Policy,
Health Resources and
Services Administration,
Public Health Service,
Room 14-22
Parklawn Building
5600 Fishers Lane
Rockville, MD 20857
(301) 443-0835
Contact: Jake Culp,
Associate Administrator

and

GRANTS MANAGEMENT

Grants Management Branch,
Bureau of Health Care
Delivery and Assistance,
Health Resources and
Services Administration,
Public Health Service,
12100 Parklawn Building
Rockville, MD 20857
(301) 443-5902
Contact: Gary Houseknecht,
Grants Management Officer

Program: Rural Health Services Outreach
(Federal program 93.912)

Description: Project grants to allow for provision of medical services to rural populations that are not receiving them. To enhance service capacity or to expand service area; to increase the depth and scope of health services in rural areas.

Restrictions: Not-for-profit, public or private entities located in non-Metropolitan Statistical Areas may apply

$ Given: Range of $50,000 - $300,000 per grant; average award is $200,000 (national figures)

Number of Awards: At least 60 awards were planned for FY91

Application Information: Program guidelines may be obtained from Program Headquarters; write or call the Grants Management Officer for application kit

Deadline: Contact Program Headquarters for deadline dates

FEDERAL GRANTS

. . . .

DEVELOPMENTAL DISABILITIES

- **ADMINISTRATION ON DEVELOPMENTAL DISABILITIES—
  BASIC SUPPORT AND ADVOCACY GRANTS**

**PROGRAM
HEADQUARTERS**
Program Operations Division,
Administration on
Developmental Disabilities,
Office of Human
Development Services,
Office of the Secretary,
Department of Health and
Human Services,
Washington, DC 20201
(202) 245-2897

Program: Administration on Developmental Disabilities—
Basic Support and Advocacy Grants (Federal program
93.630)
Description: BASIC SUPPORT PROGRAM provides formula
grants to assist states in the development of comprehensive
systems of coordinated services designed to enable persons
with developmental disabilities to reach their maximum
potential (i.e., to become independent, productive, and
integrated into their communities). PROTECTION AND
ADVOCACY PROGRAM supports states in providing
individual legal advocacy for persons with developmental
disabilities. "Developmental disability" is here defined as a
severe chronic disability of persons 5 years old or older
(and, in some cases, younger) that is attributable to mental
and/or physical impairments resulting in substantial
functional limitations—reflecting a person's lifelong need for
services.
Restrictions: Designated State agencies may apply
$ Given: Range of $350,000 - $5.1 million per award for
BASIC SUPPORT; range of $200,000 - $1.5 million per award
for PROTECTION AND ADVOCACY; average BASIC SUPPORT
award is $1.03 million; average PROTECTION AND
ADVOCACY award is $353,000 (national figures)
Number of Awards: N/A
Application Information: Program guidelines may be
obtained from Program Headquarters; for information about
funding within your state, contact your regional Department
of Health and Human Services office (see previous chapter)
Deadline: N/A
National Contact: Terence Smith, Director

. . . .

INFANTS AND TODDLERS WITH DISABILITIES

Division of Educational
Services,
Office of Special Education
Programs,
Office of the Assistant,
Secretary for Special
Education and Rehabilitative
Services,
Department of Education,
400 Maryland Avenue, S.W.
Washington, DC 20202
(202) 732-1109

Program: Infants and Toddlers with Disabilities—Early Intervention Grants (Federal program 84.181)

Description: Project grants to assist states in developing comprehensive multidisciplinary systems to provide early intervention services to disabled infants and toddlers.

Restrictions: Only states and U.S. Territories may apply; applicants with eligible projects should consult state officials for local funding procedures

$ Given: Range of $31,000 - $10,061,000 per award in 1990; average award was $1.4 million (national figures)

Number of Awards: N/A

Application Information: Forms may be obtained from the address above

Deadline: Contact the office above for current deadline information

Contact: Nancy Safer

FEDERAL GRANTS

. . . .

OTHER

EMERGENCY MEDICAL SERVICES FOR CHILDREN

PROGRAM HEADQUARTERS
Maternal and Child Health Bureau,
Health Resources and Services Administration,
Public Health Service,
Department of Health and Human Services,
Room 9-31
5600 Fishers Lane
Rockville, MD 20857
(301) 443-2250
Contact: David E. Heppel

and

GRANTS MANAGEMENT
Grants Management Branch
Maternal and Child Health Bureau,
Health Resources and Services Administration,
Public Health Service,
Department of Health and Human Services,
12300 Twinbrook Parkway
Suite 100A
Rockville, MD 20852
(301) 443-1440
Contact: Maria Carter

Program: EMS for Children (Federal program 93.127)
Description: Project grants to fund medical services that expand and improve emergency medical services for the trauma or critical care treatment of children. Priority given to projects that target specific populations, including Native Americans, minorities, and the disabled.
Restrictions: Only state governments and medical schools may apply
$ Given: Range of $53,000 - $910,000 per award; average award is $355,000 (national figures)
Number of Awards: In FY90, 11 projects were funded
Application Information: Guidelines may be obtained from Program Headquarters
Deadline: Contact Program Headquarters for current deadline information

• MATERNAL AND CHILD HEALTH-TARGETED INFANT MORTALITY INITIATIVE

**PROGRAM
HEADQUARTERS**
Maternal and Child Health
Bureau,
Health Resources and
Services Administration,
Public Health Service,
Room 9-11
Parklawn Building
5600 Fishers Lane
Rockville, MD 20857
(301) 443-2170
Contact: Dr. Vince L.
Hutchins

and

GRANTS MANAGEMENT
Maternal and Child Health
Bureau,
Health Resources and
Services Administration,
Public Health Service,
12300 Twinbrook Parkway
Suite 100A
Rockville, MD 20852
(301) 443-1440
Contact: Grants Management
Officer

Program: Healthy Start Initiative (Federal program 93.926)
Description: Project grants to reduce infant mortality rates and to improve infant health in communities with exceptionally high infant mortality rates. To improve provision of comprehensive, accessible maternity and infant health care services.
Restrictions: Eligible communities must submit proposals through an applicant designated by the chief elected official of the city/county. Applicants limited to local or state health departments and not-for-profit organizations. One application per eligible community. Application must be endorsed by the Governor of the state.
$ Given: Range of $1 million - $3 million per award (national figures)
Number of Awards: 10 grants anticipated in FY91
Application Information: Program guidelines may be obtained from Program Headquarters; for information about funding within your state, contact your regional Department of Health and Human Services office (see previous chapter)
Deadline: Contact Program Headquarters or regional DHHS office for current deadline information

FEDERAL GRANTS

• •

MATERNAL AND CHILD HEALTH SERVICES BLOCK GRANT

PROGRAM HEADQUARTERS
Maternal and Child Health
Bureau,
Health Resources and
Services Administration,
Public Health Service,
Department of Health and
Human Services,
Room 9-11
5600 Fishers Lane
Rockville, MD 20857
(301) 443-2170
Contact: Dr. Vince L.
Hutchins

and

GRANTS MANAGEMENT
Maternal and Child Health
Bureau,
Health Resources and
Services Administration,
Public Health Service,
12300 Twinbrook Parkway
Suite 100A
Rockville, MD 20852
(301) 443-1440
Contact: Waddell Avery,
Grants Management Officer

Program: Maternal and Child Health Services Block Grant
(Federal program 93.994)
Description: Formula grants to enable states to provide
health services for mothers and children who do not have
access to adequate health care. States must use at least
30% of their federal allotment for preventive and primary
care services for children, and at least 30% for services for
children with special health care needs.
Restrictions: Only states and insular areas may apply
$ Given: Range of $127,000 - $28.8 million per award;
average award is $8 million (national figures)
Number of Awards: N/A
Application Information: States may apply to Program
Headquarters for guidelines
Deadline: August 15

NATIONAL INFORMATION CENTER

**CLEARINGHOUSE ON
DISABILITY INFORMATION**
Office of Assistant Secretary
for Special Education and
Rehabilitative Services,
Department of Education
400 Maryland Avenue, S.W.
Washington, DC 20202

Description: Supplies information and directs inquiries
about various handicaps to the appropriate Federal and
national private resource organizations. Emphasis on service
providers and relevant Federal legislation. Written requests
and telephone requests accepted. Publications made
available to the public on request at no charge.
Contact: Carolyn Corlett, (202) 732-1242; or Donald Barrett,
(202) 732-1245

Index

· · · · · · · · · · · · · · · · · · · ·

COMPANIES/CORPORATIONS

Books in Laurie Blum's **Free Money** Series

• •

THE FREE MONEY FOR CHILD CARE SERIES

Free Money for Day Care
• Advice on finding financial aid for family day care, child care centers, in-house care, and camp and summer programs

Free Money for Private Schools
• Where to find money for preschool and nursery education, private primary schools, and private secondary schools

Free Money for Children's Medical and Dental Care
• Ways to receive money for both long- and short-term medical care, dental and orthodontic treatment, and dermatological procedures

Free Money for Behavioral and Genetic Childhood Disorders
• Free Money for treatment of learning disabilities, eating disorders, retardation, alcohol and drug abuse, neurological disturbances, and sleep disorders

THE FREE MONEY FOR HEALTH CARE SERIES

Free Money for Diseases of Aging
• Find money to help pay for major surgery and medical care for diseases of aging such as Alzheimer's, Parkinson's, stroke, and other chronic illnesses

Free Money for Heart Disease and Cancer Care
• Ways to receive money for the diagnosis and treatment (surgery or long-term care) of cancer and heart disease

Free Money for Fertility Treatments
• Where to look for Free Money for infertility testing, treatment, insemination, and preliminary adoption expenses

Free Money for the Care and Treatment of Mental and Emotional Disorders
• Detailed guidance on locating Free Money for psychological care